The Soul of THE LION, THE WITCH, & THE WARDROBE

Gene Veith

Victor®

The Bible Teacher's Teacher

COOK COMMUNICATIONS MINISTRIES
Colorado Springs, Colorado • Paris, Ontario
KINGSWAY COMMUNICATIONS LTD
Eastbourne, England

Victor® is an imprint of
Cook Communications Ministries, Colorado Springs, CO 80918
Cook Communications, Paris, Ontario
Kingsway Communications, Eastbourne, England

THE SOUL OF THE LION, THE WITCH AND THE WARDROBE
© 2005 by Gene Edward Veith Jr.

Published in association with the literary agency of Jan P. Dennis, 19350 Glen
Hollow Circle, Monument, CO 80132.

Cover Design: BMB Design/Scott Johnson
Cover Illustration: Ron Adair

First Printing, 2005
Printed in Canada

Printing/Year
1 2 3 4 5 6 7 8 9 10 / 10 09 08 07 06 05

Unless otherwise noted, Scripture quotations are taken from The Holy Bible:
English Standard Version. Copyright © 2001 by The Standard Bible Society, 1300
Crescent Street, Wheaton, IL 60187, a division of Crossway Bibles. Used by permission. Scripture quotations marked KJV are taken from the *King James Version* of
the Bible. Italics in Scripture have been added by the author for emphasis.

ISBN 0781442125

To Paul, Joanna, and Mary,
who recognized who Aslan was

Visit www.thesoulofthelion.com for additional powerful teaching and study resources.

CONTENTS

PREFACE

This book is a companion to *The Lion, the Witch and the Wardrobe* that will help you unpack the meaning of the story. It also shows how this book by C. S. Lewis fits in with the whole heritage of Christian literature, particularly that form to which many Christian writers have gravitated: fantasy.

Today, fantasy, though pioneered by Christian authors, has taken some other turns. *The Chronicles of Narnia* have never been more popular, and since the stories have now broken through onto the silver screen, they will probably become more popular still. But there are two other wildly popular fantasy series that also are being made into movies: *Harry Potter* and *His Dark Materials*. This book shows how the Narnia fantasies are quite different from these others.

The books in the *His Dark Materials* series by Philip Pullman were written specifically to counter *The Chronicles of Narnia* and to persuade its young readers toward atheism, just as the Narnia books persuade them toward Christianity. So a comparison of these two, not just as books but in what they reveal about the worldviews that they are seeking to communicate, is especially important.

This book has two parts. The first part, The Story, is simply an exposition of the story of *The Lion, the Witch and the Wardrobe*. It opens up its symbolism and themes, as well as some of the more subtle details of what is going on in the story.

The second part, The Fantasy Wars, delves into the larger issues regarding Christian (and also non-Christian and even anti-Christian) fantasy.

The two parts may be read consecutively, or you may

choose to read one or the other separately. You don't have to read the whole book, though it will be helpful if you do, simply because a solid grounding in Narnia will prepare you for the next section. But the book is written as a resource, as well as a connected discussion.

It is also written to help you think through the story yourself, whether alone or as part of a group. If you have read *The Lion, the Witch and the Wardrobe,* seen the movie, or are studying the book at home, at school, or in a Bible study class, this book can help you discover its depths. To help guide your reflections, study questions have been added at the back of the book, which you can either think about yourself or, even better, talk through with other people who have also read—or seen—the story.

Special thanks goes to Mark Joseph of Walden Media, a company devoted to the production of positive movies for children and families, including the movie *The Chronicles of Narnia: The Lion, the Witch and the Wardrobe.* It was Mark who encouraged me to write this book.

Thanks, too, to Jan Dennis, Jimmy Peacock, and the people at Cook Communications, in particular Craig Bubeck, who supported and promoted this project with such enthusiasm. And extra-special Narnian thanks goes to my wife, Jackquelyn, who by her own initiative and out of her own considerate and loving heart took on my household chores—to the point of even mowing the grass—to enable me to meet a tight deadline.

And thanks, too, to our now-grown children—Paul, Joanna, and Mary—to whom I read *The Lion, the Witch and the Wardrobe* so often, and then they read it to me, so that I came to know it well.

STEALING PAST WATCHFUL DRAGONS

The Lion, the Witch and the Wardrobe had its beginnings, C. S. Lewis said, in a picture that kept running through his head from the time he was sixteen years old: a faun (half-goat and half-man) in a snowy forest holding an umbrella and carrying packages. When he was about forty years old, Lewis decided to write a story about it.[1]

Other pictures came bubbling and boiling, as he put it, into his mind: a queen on a sleigh, a lamppost in the woods. Then a lion, he said, came bounding into it all. When the lion came, the story all started to come together.

He began with these mental pictures, he said; but to make a story out of them, he next needed a form. What kind of story could contain a faun, a queen, a lamppost, and a lion? A fairy tale, of course. That form, in turn, has rules of its own that he would have to follow: The writing would have to be brief and to the point. The fairy-tale form likewise has traditions that he would have to follow, and yet it is also flexible, capable of covering a lot of territory. The vocabulary, though, would be limited. As he began writing, Lewis said that he fell in love with the fairy-tale form, appreciating its difficulties like a sculptor appreciates the hardness of the stone.[2]

> There is nothing more marvelous than the truths of Christianity. So why do so many people think they are boring?

But then the story acquired a larger purpose. Lewis had become a Christian as an adult. All of his life, he had felt a deep yearning, even though he did not know what he was yearning for. After a long time, he learned about the God who created the world, who came into that world in the flesh as the God-man Jesus Christ, who rescued us from Satan by dying for our sins, who rose from the dead to give us a new and everlasting life through the Holy Spirit. The Christian faith fulfilled all of his yearnings. The truths of the Bible were mind-blowing, so amazingly wonderful that for awhile he thought they must be too good to be true. Only when he stopped fighting God and believed Christ did he realize that they were true all the same.

There is nothing more marvelous than the truths of Christianity. So why do so many people think they are boring? How is it that even believers sometimes treat theology as if it were uninteresting, dull, irrelevant? How can anyone be less than excited about the mysteries of the Trinity, the incarnation, the atonement, the kingdom of Heaven, the rich and complex and beautiful view of reality that is opened up by the Christian worldview?

By the time Lewis started on his fairy tale, he had already become a remarkably effective apologist for the Christian faith. Part of his effectiveness came from his ability to show readers that there is more to Christianity than they have perhaps realized. In books such as *Mere Christianity*, he not only makes a persuasive case that Christianity is true, he also shows just how rich and full the Christian faith can be to those who have previously taken it for granted or have never taken it seriously.

Lewis remembered how, as a child, he was taken to church. There he did learn about Jesus. But how, he wondered, could he have missed the magnitude of who Jesus is and what Jesus had accomplished for him? He realized that he had been told how he ought to feel about, say, the sufferings of Christ. And yet, that very sense of obligation, he thought, can freeze out a genuine emotional response. Plus, he was taught to approach the stories of the Bible with so much reverence that they were distanced from his real life.

As Lewis was piecing together his imaginative pictures of the faun, the witch, the lamppost, and the lion into a fairy tale, a thought occurred to him. Perhaps his story could break through the inhibitions, misunderstandings, and false connotations that often block children—and adults—from coming to terms with the Christian message. "Supposing that by casting all these things into an imaginary world, stripping them of their stained-glass and Sunday school associations, one could make them for the first time appear in their potency? Could one not thus steal past those watchful dragons?"[3]

In a letter, he went so far as to say that "the fairy-tale version of the Passion in The Lion, etc. works ... because—tho' this sounds odd—it bypasses one's reverence and piety."[4]

Lewis was certainly not against stained glass or Sunday school or reverence or piety. His point was that he wanted to present the Christian story in a fresh way, to get past the defenses of those who think they have heard it all before, who are so familiar with Bible stories that they no longer notice how amazing they are. He wanted to present spiritual truths in such a way that they sneak by "the watchful dragons" that are on guard against them.

His method was to make his fairy tale into a wondrous fantasy that had as its meaning spiritual reality.

The Lion, the Witch and the Wardrobe was published in 1950. Lewis kept writing stories about the world he created until he had written the seven titles in *The Chronicles of Narnia*. They have sold millions and millions of copies, becoming favorites of children and adults alike. And now that *The Lion, the Witch and the Wardrobe* is being turned into a major motion picture, even more people of all ages will be drawn into this world, whose message may well sneak past their "dragons."

Baptizing the Imagination

Lewis said that a key event in his own journey from atheism to faith was happening to pick up a book that caught his eye in a bookstall at a train station. Titled *Phantastes*, it was written by the nineteenth-century Christian author George MacDonald. Some readers today find it captivating, while others are totally bewildered by it. But for Lewis, this work of fantasy had a dramatic effect. He said that reading that book gave him a glimpse of something beyond the train station and his own grubby life, a sense of something good and mysterious and powerful, and, without his knowing what it was, the book made him yearn for it. Later, he said, he realized that the book was giving him his first experience of a sense of holiness. As he put it, *Phantastes* baptized his imagination.[5]

It would be years later before Lewis came to believe that Jesus was the Son of God and trusted Christ as his Savior. This happened in large measure thanks to the witnessing of his good friend J. R. R. Tolkien, another great fantasy writer and the author of *The Lord of the Rings*. But Lewis believed that reading the fairy tale by George MacDonald that he just happened to pick up in a train station long ago played a role in his spiritual pilgrimage.

> Our imagination is simply our amazing ability to conjure up images in our minds.

Many readers could say the same about *The Lion, the Witch and the Wardrobe*. Lewis's books have helped bring untold numbers of people to faith and have helped even more to hold on to that faith and to grow spiritually. Some cite his apologetic books (besides *Mere Christianity*, titles such as *The Problem of Pain, Miracles, God in the Dock*) as having had a profound impact on their lives. Others cite the influence of his fiction, including his most popular, biggest-selling books of all, *The Chronicles of Narnia*.

How can that be? Surely Christianity must be about truth, not fantasy. Faith is not just some inner mystical feeling. Rather, it is a relationship with Christ, based on what he did for us on the cross, as revealed in God's Word. That is to say, genuine faith is grounded in something other than the self. It is *extra nos*, as the theologians say, meaning "outside the self." Faith is a connection with the objective reality of Christ and what he achieved for us at Calvary. Genuine faith is not just a matter of something inside our heads. Surely some fantasy, a made-up story that appeals to our imagination, can have nothing to do with true faith. In fact, deriving our beliefs from fantasy is surely dangerous, a formula for idolatry rather than the true faith.

It is certainly true that many people have a fantasy religion, a self-made theology that is dreamed up according to their desires but that exists only in their heads. Lewis himself, more than almost anyone else, battled these kinds of delusions and idolatries. In his nonfiction—and, I would say, even in his fantasies—his message was always that Christianity is not simply something we make up for ourselves, some inner construction that makes us feel better. Rather, he always insisted and argued and demonstrated that Christianity is objectively true.

But here is why our imagination does need to be baptized. The word "imagination" does not mean simply making things up. Nor does it have anything to do with being creative, as when artsy types make excuses for themselves and try to impress us by insisting on how "imaginative" they are. Rather, the word "imagination" refers to a power that we all have, one that we nearly always take for granted, despite how astonishing it really is.

Our imagination is simply our amazing ability to conjure up images in our minds. I say the word "tree," and you can think of a tree. I say the term "Christmas tree," and you can picture one in all of its colors, decorations, and lights. You can even imagine how it smells. You can also bring in all of your memories (that time when you were six that you found that favorite toy from your parents under that tree) and the personal associations that come along with the Christmas tree (how you miss that old house where you would put up the tree in the center of the room, back before the death in the family or the divorce or whatever, as your imagination brings back all of the memories).

We do not think just in ideas or abstractions; we also think with our imagination. That is, we think in images, in tangible details that partake of our senses, even though we are only contemplating them in our mind. Our language, let alone our literature, depends on metaphors. We use metaphors even when we think in abstractions, as when we speak of "grasping" an idea (a metaphor of a hand grabbing on to something) or "comprehending" a concept (which is simply based on the Latin word for grasping with the hand).[6]

Our powers of imagination include the astounding ability God has given us to call up experiences from the past. This is called memory. (Think of a tree you used to climb or play around.)[7] We can imagine what we are going to do in the future. (Think about how the leaves of that tree will change colors in the fall, and how you will then be raking them.) We can even imagine things that do not exist except as something we have created in our mind. (Think of a tree. Then make it blue. Now plaid.)

The imagination needs training just as the intellect does. When we read, we exercise our imagination, picturing what is happening as we process the author's words. With television and movies, someone else has imagined the story for us, but when the imagery is done well, the pictures and responses can enter into our own imagination. "Having a good imagination," as we say, is a function of creativity (in the sense of "creating" something in our mind, which applies just as well to business, science, and practical planning as to the arts). A good imagination (that is, the ability to conjure up things in the mind with facility) is part and parcel of our mental ability. It is thus important to exercise our imagination in order to strengthen our mind. One way to do so is simply by reading books, which can make us smarter, just as lifting weights can make us stronger.

We have a problem though. While the imagination is simply one of the powers God has given us (and it works so naturally and smoothly that we often do not even realize how odd and miraculous it is), we are still fallen creatures. All of our powers, including both our reasoning ability and our imagining ability, have become limited and twisted by sin.

> We need to be able to imagine sharp moral distinctions to help us navigate in a morally mixed-up world.

We can use this power of the imagination for planning, problem solving, and creativity. We can also use our imagination for daydreams of lust, hate, revenge, and wallowing in self-pity. The images we take in from the outside from movies, television and radio, the Internet, music, books, and periodicals can extend our experience and our reflection in positive ways; but sometimes the images they create in our mind do not help us, filling our mind instead with sinful desires and evil fantasies. This is a problem because Jesus himself tells us that our sinfulness consists not only in what we do, but also in what we think (Matt. 5:21–28). The Bible tells us that just before the great flood that destroyed all mankind, "God saw that the wickedness of man was great in the earth, and that every imagination of the thoughts of his heart was only evil continually" (Gen. 6:5 KJV).

Another problem with the fallen imagination is that it is limited. Many people cannot picture what goodness is, much less emulate virtue in their actions; they get goodness all muddled up with evil. Many people, especially today, are so conditioned by the narrow, materialistic worldview of their times that they cannot imagine any kind of spiritual reality beyond their physical senses.

> "I am aiming at a sort of pre-baptism of the child's imagination."

This is why positive works of the imagination—such as *The Lion, the Witch and the Wardrobe*—can be so helpful in the discipleship of the mind. They provoke in our mind helpful images. The best fantasies can give us images of goodness—virtues such as courage and self-sacrifice—and render them attractive, making them something to which we can aspire. Fantasies tend to have great clarity when it comes to good and evil.

It is true that in this fallen real world, moral issues are often confusing and unclear. We do not always know for sure who is the "good guy" and who is the "bad guy" in real life, so that we often have to deal (as they say) with shades of gray. In fantasy, though, the blacks and whites are sharp and vivid, and the conflict between them is heightened. Experts have pointed out that stories—particularly fantasy stories such as fairy tales—are especially helpful in teaching virtuous behavior, more so than mere abstract precepts and much more so than slice-of-life, intrinsically ambiguous moral dilemmas.[8] We need to be able to imagine sharp moral distinctions to help us navigate in a morally mixed-up world.

The best fantasies can also help form our conscience by presenting their subject matter in such a way that we are attracted to what is good. Just as important, they present their subject matter so that we are repelled by what is evil. This process reverses what tends to be the case in our fallen condition. In our sinful state of mind, we tend rather to be attracted to what is evil and are sometimes repelled by what is good. Bad fantasies exploit this tendency by ridiculing virtue and presenting evil behavior as something to look up to. They make us yearn to do these evil things ourselves, if only in our imagination, but perhaps even in real life if we get the chance. Positive fantasies, on the other hand, help us cultivate desires that accord with virtue rather than sin.

Notice that a fantasy, to be helpful morally, dares not ignore evil or present only good images. All plots have to have conflict. Goodness has to have something to oppose and to overcome. A story consisting only of sunshiny goodness can create the impression that "everything is beautiful [that is, good] in its own way"—a sentimental and false view of life that, however moralistic it may seem, is certainly not Christian. The best fantasies recognize the reality of darkness and make evil repellent, as something we should not want to imitate but rather to resist.

Fantasies such as *The Lion, the Witch and the Wardrobe* also help us to imagine a realm beyond the narrow confines of this all-too-solid world that so often seems to be all there is, nothing more than drab material without meaning

> We have the example of Jesus Christ himself, who never sinned, but who explained the kingdom of God by means of parables.

or hope. The best fantasies give us inklings that there is something more to existence, something beautiful and unearthly, perhaps a foretaste of our true spiritual home, a glimpse of holiness. This is what *Phantastes* did for C. S. Lewis, baptizing his imagination.

In our current culture, oblivious as it is to either moral or spiritual realities, a good imagination—not just a strong imagination, but a sanctified imagination—can be a spiritual survival skill.

George Sayer, Lewis's close friend who later became his biographer, reports on what Lewis intended as the purpose of *The Chronicles of Narnia*:

> His idea, as he once explained it to me, was to make it easier for children to accept Christianity when they met it later in life. He hoped that they would be vaguely reminded of the somewhat similar stories that they had read and enjoyed years before. "I am aiming at a sort of pre-baptism of the child's imagination."[9]

That is to say, Lewis wanted to do for children what *Phantastes* had done for him, to shape their imagination so that they could grasp Christianity when they heard about it, despite the "dragons" that might get in their way.

The Bible and the Imagination

Of course, the spiritual realm does have to do with a reality that cannot be seen (Heb. 11:1). For many people, the great concepts of Christianity—faith, grace, justification, eternal life—are just words. They are abstractions, "big ideas" that are little more than concepts, rather than living truths. As teachers know, the way to explain just about any abstract concept is to bring it down to earth by using an example, illustrating the idea by means of something tangible.

In the Bible, God reveals himself to us not just with theological statements—though there are some of those, as in the epistles of Paul—but with stories. The Bible largely consists of true stories of history: what God did when he created the universe; what happened with Adam and Eve; the actions of Abraham and his children; the account of the slavery in Egypt and how God delivered his people; the victories and the sins of the judges and the kings; the repeated cycles of judgment and redemption, exile and return. Then the New Testament gives us the Gospels: four books recounting the life, death, and resurrection of Christ. Then come the Acts—that is, the actions—of his apostles. After the Epistles, an interlude of inspired letters to the churches, including historical references and contexts, we have the book of Revelation, a description of the last days, with hair-raising images of tribulations and monsters, culminating in the triumphant return of Christ.

Within these historical narratives (a kind of writing that depicts an unfolding action), God's Word assumes the form of other kinds of literature, such as the poetry of the Psalms and Prophets. Poetry is a kind of writing that communicates largely through highly vivid imagery: "The LORD is my shepherd" (Ps. 23:1); "The rivers clap their hands" (Ps. 98:8); "[The person grounded in God's Word is] like a tree planted by streams of water" (Ps. 1:3). Poetry directly addresses and calls upon the human imagination. The poems in the Bible are no exception. Indeed, they are poetry of the highest power.

The stories in the Bible, though they are read and comprehended by the imagination, are histories. The Bible gives precedent for true stories. Some people may wonder if it is appropriate to communicate spiritual truths by means of fiction (stories about imagined, not actual, events). But the Bible gives precedent for fictional stories as well. We have the example of Jesus Christ himself, who never sinned, but who explained the kingdom of God by means of parables. A parable is a fictional story that illustrates some point.

Notice that a parable and other kinds of fiction can nevertheless be true: The *meaning* is true. The incidents they set forth exist only in the imagination—which is a kind of real existence—but they illustrate and make the case for truth in the real world. Fantasies can do the same (as we will see with *The Lion, the Witch and the Wardrobe*).

Jesus said that the kingdom of God is like a man who sows good seed in his field while his enemy sows weeds there; it is like a mustard seed; like the yeast a woman uses to bake bread; like a treasure hidden in a field; like a merchant searching for pearls; like a net thrown into the sea. (These are all from just one chapter, Matthew 13).

Jesus used parables so much when teaching people that, according to the gospel of Mark, "he did not speak to them without a parable" (4:34).

Jesus himself and his work to win our salvation are themselves subjects of a particular kind of idea-communicating imagery called a symbol. When the children of Israel in the Old Testament killed a spotless lamb and brought its blood into the sanctuary as an atonement offering for the sins of the people, they were dramatizing and symbolizing the redemption carried out by Jesus, "the Lamb of God, who takes away the sin of the world!" (John 1:29). The bronze serpent lifted up by Moses for the healing of the people from the punishment due their sins symbolizes Christ and the sin he bore as he was lifted up on the cross (John 3:14).

Christ is also described as a shoot (Isa. 11:1), a branch (Jer. 23:5), a rock (1 Cor. 10:4), a cornerstone (1 Peter 2:7), a stumbling block (1 Cor. 1:23), and a door (John 10:9). And in the same chapter in the book of Revelation in which Christ is described as "a Lamb standing, as though it had been slain" (5:6), he is also depicted as another animal: "Behold, the Lion of the tribe of Judah, the Root of David, has conquered" (v. 5).

WHERE DOES NARNIA BEGIN?

Choosing a reading sequence:

The Chronicles of Narnia are sometimes read in different orders. Here is the order of publication, which is the sequence that earlier editions followed:

1. *The Lion, the Witch and the Wardrobe* (1950)
2. *Prince Caspian* (1951)
3. *The Voyage of the Dawn Treader* (1952)
4. *The Silver Chair* (1953)
5. *The Horse and His Boy* (1954)
6. *The Magician's Nephew* (1955)
7. *The Last Battle* (1956)

As Lewis developed his world into a coherent and unified whole, he told in the next to the last book he wrote, *The Magician's Nephew*, about its creation by Aslan, its first human visitors, how the witch entered in, and how the lamppost, the wardrobe, and other details about Narnia came to be. This, plus putting the other books in order with the history of Narnia they recount, made another way of reading the series—in chronological order, which is the sequence given in the more recent editions:

1. *The Magician's Nephew*
2. *The Lion, the Witch and the Wardrobe*
3. *The Horse and His Boy*
4. *Prince Caspian*
5. *The Voyage of the Dawn Treader*
6. *The Silver Chair*
7. *The Last Battle*

For those interested in watching how Lewis's ideas about Narnia developed and grew, an even better order to read them in is the order in which Lewis wrote them, which is slightly different yet from the order of publication:

1. *The Lion, the Witch and the Wardrobe*
2. *Prince Caspian*
3. *The Voyage of the Dawn Treader*
4. *The Horse and His Boy*
5. *The Silver Chair*
6. *The Magician's Nephew*
7. *The Last Battle*

Andrew Rilstone has a good discussion of the different orders at http://www.aslan.demon.co.uk/narnia.htm.

PART I:

THE STORY

CHAPTER 1

NARNIA

Creation and Sub-creation

Perhaps when you were little you played in an old house with lots of nooks and crannies, climbing around the boxes in the attic, hiding in the closets, and letting your imagination go wild. That is how *The Lion, the Witch and the Wardrobe* gets started, with four children (Lucy, Edmund, Susan, and Peter) playing in an old house on a rainy day. Lucy goes inside a wardrobe (a large chest used for hanging clothes before the advent of built-in closets).

She enjoys the feel of the old fur coats and burrows in (careful, being safety-minded, not to close the door). She keeps going farther back, until the fur feels prickly, like pine needles, and she notices she is walking on something soft and cold. She sees a light, which turns out to be a lamppost. She sees that she is in a snowy wood. When she gets to the lamppost, she sees a faun with a scarf around his neck, fumbling with an umbrella and packages. She then realizes that she is in another world.

This world, which she learns is called Narnia, is inhabited by talking animals. And, in addition to the faun, there are centaurs (creatures that are half-man and half-horse), nymphs, dryads, giants, elfish and fairylike beings, dwarves, and dragons. As the story unfolds, we see that it is a medieval world, with kings and queens and knights, castles and towers and chivalry.

> They enter a world of moral testing, high dangers, weighty responsibilities, and spiritual trials.

Narnia is a wonderful fantasy world on one level, but it is not an escapist kind of fantasy. Later on, when all four of the children leave their world, where adults have taken care of them, and make their way into Narnia, they enter a world of moral testing, high dangers, weighty responsibilities, and spiritual trials.

Nor is Narnia, a self-contained fantasy world, unconnected to the "real life" of earth. The children travel back and forth between the two worlds and learn that the two are both parallel and connected. The spiritual and moral laws of earth are the same as for Narnia, where they are heightened and clarified.

So what are we to make of this fantasy world? What does Narnia mean?

The World Inside

After her first visit to Narnia alone, Lucy comes back and joins the others, who do not believe at first that she has been to another world. Later, when Edmund, Susan, and Peter go into the wardrobe with Lucy and enter Narnia for the first time, they all realize they are not dressed for the snow and the cold weather. But the wardrobe is full of fur coats, stored with mothballs. All the children need to do to dress themselves for the cold of the Narnian winter is to simply borrow some of the fur coats hanging in the wardrobe. Peter, though, worries whether this is the right thing to do, since the coats do not belong to them.

Susan points out that they will not even be taking the coats out of the wardrobe. Peter comes to agree that no one can accuse them of stealing the coats since they will be leaving them in the wardrobe right where they found them. "I suppose," he said, "this whole country is in the wardrobe."[1] And then off they go, wearing the coats, into the vast recesses of Narnia.

This is an effective imaginative device: a structure that is small on the outside, but which, on the inside, contains immense space. As Lewis puts it in *The Last Battle*, the inside is bigger than the outside.[2]

Other writers have played with this same device. "I could be bounded in a nutshell," says Hamlet, "and count myself a king of infinite space."[3] To jump ahead several centuries, in the popular British sci-fi TV thriller, *Dr. Who*, his TARDIS looks like a police call box, the size of an old-fashioned telephone booth. But inside, it is a gigantic space-and-time ship, with multiple levels, huge storage facilities, and untold numbers of compartments.

Perhaps the first in English literature to dream up such a curious structure was Edmund Spenser, the sixteenth-century author of *The Faerie Queene*, another symbolic fantasy. It was one of Lewis's favorite books. In his profession as a literary scholar at Oxford and Cambridge, Lewis made a reputation for himself as an expert on Spenser and *The Faerie Queene*. At one point in that poem, the Red Cross Knight goes up to a small, broken-down hovel, the sort of hut in which a peasant might live. He stoops to go inside, whereupon he finds himself inside a spacious and magnificent palace. He learns that he has entered the House of Holiness.[4]

Just looking at it from the outside, the House of Holiness looks humble, narrow, even unattractive. But from within, the House of Holiness is wonderful, vast, and liberating. Spenser was symbolizing the true church and the nature of true faith. Looked at in purely external terms, the church may not seem like much—it appears weak, off-putting, austere, something to be scorned and looked down upon. And yet, from *within* the church, from the perspective of those who have come to know Christ, the church is marvelous, a place where God is present with his gifts of life and salvation, a place not at all of restrictions (as the world thinks) but of freedom and joy.

In terms of Spenser's story, this is exactly what his main character, the Red Cross Knight, needs to learn. He has been judging by appearances, chasing after every false religion that seems so attractive and yet leads him into bondage, falsehood, and despair. He has abandoned faithful Una in favor of the beautiful Duessa (who is actually an evil witch), trusting the pious-appearing Archimago (who is actually an evil wizard). The Red Cross Knight has been living in the House of Pride, which is the opposite of the House of Holiness: spectacular-looking on the outside, but small and fake and empty within.

The tendency of the Red Cross Knight up to this point has been to go after things that have a flashy appearance but in reality are superficial, insubstantial, and seductive. The House of Holiness is the opposite of all these things: Despite its unpromising appearance, reality dwells there. The Red Cross Knight must go to the House of Holiness—where he learns repentance, the Word of God, and the grace of Christ—in order to be restored and to regain his strength to face his final trial.

The figure of a small vessel that contains infinity also spoke to Lewis of Christ. In *The Last Battle*, the finale of *The Chronicles of Narnia*, there is a stable. From the outside, it is a shack, seemingly a place of imprisonment that supposedly contains something hideous. Lucy, who makes a reappearance in that book, and some friends are captured by the villains and thrown into the stable. "They were inside a little thatched stable, about twelve feet long and six feet wide."5 But once inside the shack, the friends discover that it is like they are outdoors, with green grass, a forest with fruit trees, and a deep blue sky overhead. The door is still standing, and they can look through a peephole and see their enemies

"In our world too, a Stable once had something inside it that was bigger than our whole world."

exulting over their prisoners. The company inside the enclosure discusses the curious phenomenon:

> "It seems then," said Tirian, smiling himself, "that the Stable seen from within and the Stable seen from without are two different places."
> "Yes," said the Lord Digory. "Its inside is bigger than its outside."
> "Yes," said Queen Lucy. "In our world too, a Stable once had something inside it that was bigger than our whole world."[6]

She was referring to the manger in Bethlehem, which held God Incarnate, a little baby who held the whole universe in his hand.

Narnia of the Imagination

There is another sense in which the inside is bigger than the outside. There actually is—in ordinary life, not just in a story or a symbol—a physically small object that contains vast and measureless worlds. It is called a human being.

Consider yourself. As a physical package, you are probably somewhat less than the size of a wardrobe. And yet, you yourself are a universe of thoughts, feelings, memories, and dreams. You are full of

> Appearances aside, that person is, in fact, a universe of thoughts and feelings, an immortal soul, just as you and I are.

contradictions, moral struggles, feelings of guilt and happiness, plans for the future, private secrets, and your own imaginings. You are also an immortal soul, a spiritual being designed for an astounding eternal life, with a relationship with God himself.

Consider someone else, a person you can see across the room or out the window. He or she, too, may seem like just a physical object, perhaps with an unattractive face or a fat body, a style totally lacking in "coolness." (Sometimes we treat people as objects, as things we use for our own purposes.) But, appearances aside, that person is, in fact, a universe of thoughts and feelings, an immortal soul, just as you and I are.

So Narnia, on one level, is analogous to the life of the mind, which runs parallel to the physical life we lead. It represents the realm of the imagination.

Notice how Narnia contains elements drawn from a wide spectrum of other imaginative literature. Fauns come from Roman folklore. Centaurs, nymphs, and dryads come from Greek mythology. Dwarves and giants come from Germanic mythology. The elfish and fairylike beings come from British folklore. The kings and queens and knights come from the medieval tales that still fascinate us, as witness the continued use of swords and armor in science-fiction movies and video games. Talking animals are staples of children's stories from Aesop's fables to Mickey Mouse cartoons.

In the Narnia stories, there is a connection between what the children have read in their storybooks and this strange world in which they find themselves. Later in the story, Peter trusts a robin that leads them to Mr. Beaver, because robins are good birds in all the stories he has read. In a later Narnia book, *The Voyage of the Dawn Treader*, the obnoxious Eustace is disadvantaged when it comes to dragons and other things he is encountering in Narnia

The closest real-world equivalent of going through a wardrobe into a marvelous world is opening a book.

because he has read all the wrong books. Eustace prefers to read about materialistic things like grain elevators rather than books that are really practical, namely, fairy tales. And since Eustace—his imagination and his conscience remaining unformed—does not know much about dragons, he turns into one.

It should be noted, though, that the legendary creatures who live in Narnia think that *we* are legendary. For them, *our* world is the realm of myths and legends, as is evident in the book on the faun's shelf: *Men, Monks, and Gamekeepers: A Study in Popular Legend, or, Is Man a Myth?*

The point is, Narnia points to the realm of the human imagination. Thus, the closest real-world equivalent of going through a wardrobe into a marvelous world is opening a book.

Narnia as Literary Fantasy

Actually, we learn later in the other books, each of which has a different way of getting there, that Narnia is not inside the wardrobe. The wardrobe is more of a threshold into this other world. The fantasy world of Narnia is, in fact, parallel to the realistic world of England during World War II. The children go back and forth between both worlds.

Both of the books' settings, the fantastic and the realistic, are fictional and thus imaginary, of course. Lucy and the people she meets in the realistic world, such as the Professor and Mrs. Macready the housekeeper, are just as much fictional creations as the "imaginary" characters she meets in the fantasy world, such as the White Witch and the talking beaver, even though the "realistic" part of the book seems to portray things that could actually happen and that do actually happen (evacuating a city during wartime; a brother tormenting his sister; children playing in a big house). Both the fantasy setting and the realistic setting are parallel to our actual, real-life world that you, the reader, and I, the writer of this book, actually inhabit. That is to say, in *The Lion, the Witch and the Wardrobe*, C. S. Lewis sets up three levels that work together: the fantastic, the realistic, and the real.

Authors have played around with such levels of fictionality for centuries. They have found that fantasy is actually a good genre with which to explore real-world truth.

Lewis's fantasy, with its two worlds, is different from that of his close friend J. R. R. Tolkien, author of *The Lord of the Rings*. With Middle Earth, the setting of that work, Tolkien created a completely self-contained imaginative universe. Tolkien not only wrote one of the greatest fantasies ever conceived, he also wrote one of the greatest critical discussions about fantasies ever produced.[7]

In his essay *On Fairy Stories*, Tolkien said that the imaginary universe conjured up by the author is a "sub-creation." Just as God created the real universe, a human author, who bears God's image, has an analogous power of being creative. There is a rather huge difference, of course, between a creative author and the creator God. The human creator depends on what God has already created (colors, shapes, nature, people). More dramatically, when a human author creates a world, it exists only in the writer's imagination and that of his readers. But when God creates a world, it actually exists.

Thus, for Tolkien, fantasy is distinct from what really exists, but it is nevertheless a sign of, and a tribute to, the work of God. Tolkien's stories are filled with meaning and with themes that illuminate life in the real world. But Middle Earth is another world, completely separate from ours, with its own natural laws and its own unique inhabitants, an imaginative entity unto itself.

That is why Tolkien disliked allegory, a fantasy written to symbolize truths in the real world. Tolkien's approach has inspired many other fantasy writers. Lewis, though, while influenced by Tolkien, wrote a different kind of fantasy. Again, he had two worlds—the realistic and the fantasy—going on side by side. Also, Lewis liked allegory.

> "The function of allegory is not to hide but to reveal, and it is properly used only for that which cannot be said, or so well said, in literal speech."

C. S. Lewis's first book is titled *The Allegory of Love*. Basically his graduate school dissertation, the book explored—in a fresh, original way that established his reputation as a literary scholar—a number of medieval love poems. Lewis showed how the poets who composed these works explored the experience and the ideals of love by writing allegories, that is, stories that consist of symbols.

The high point of the love allegory, according to the young Oxford tutor, came with Edmund Spenser and his *Faerie Queene*. As has been seen, this work is also an allegory about the Christian faith.

Christian authors have long been attracted to allegory as a way to write about their faith. A symbol expresses an idea in terms of a tangible image. A symbolic story allows its writer to put these ideas into motion and explore them in depth.

> The function of allegory is not to hide but to reveal, and it is properly used only for that which cannot be said, or so well said, in literal speech. The inner life, and specially the life of love, religion, and spiritual adventure, has therefore always been the field of true allegory; for here there are intangibles which only allegory can fix and reticences which only allegory can overcome.[8]

In *The Divine Comedy*, Dante describes the torments of hell as symbols of the sins they punish. (The wrathful tear each other apart in a river of blood; those who sin against love are frozen in their own isolation—just as they did and were on earth.) John Bunyan's *Pilgrim's Progress* is the great Protestant allegory, showing Christian slogging his way through the Slough of Despond (i.e., the swamp of depression), being tempted and persecuted at Vanity Fair, and losing his burden at the Strait Gate of the Cross.

The model for Narnia, though, was Spenser's Faerie Land. This, too, is a parallel world, with the hero—King Arthur while he was still a prince—crossing over from one world to the other. Faerie Land, too, is populated by a grab bag of creatures from folklore, legends, and classical mythology. Faerie

> For *The Lion, the Witch and the Wardrobe*, the symbolic center is the sacrifice of Aslan on the stone table for the sins of Edmund.

Land is an allegory, but even it will set aside the point-by-point symbolism for a while to indulge in sheer adventure.

In *The Allegory of Love*, Lewis points out that each of the six books of Spenser's long but unfinished narrative poem has one scene that embodies the theme of the whole book, its "allegorical core," the symbolic center around which the whole story is built and which provides the key for its interpretation.[9]

The Chronicles of Narnia are not full-fledged, point-by-point allegories as such.[10] Still, Lewis follows Spenser in giving each novel an "allegorical core." For *The Lion, the Witch and the Wardrobe,* as we shall see, the symbolic center is the sacrifice of Aslan on the Stone Table for the sins of Edmund.

CHAPTER 2

SONS OF ADAM AND DAUGHTERS OF EVE

Human Nature in Two Worlds

One reason young people appreciate *The Chronicles of Narnia* is that they can tell the author understands them and what they go through in their lives. The writers of many children's books talk down to their readers, all of that cuteness and joyous innocence reflecting adults' sentimental ideals about childhood, rather than what childhood is really like.

In *The Chronicles of Narnia*, though, young readers—or viewers—recognize characters like themselves who have to put up with bullying, betrayals, bad schools, and the overall cruelty that children often show to each other. C. S. Lewis's stories also show children having to make hard choices, coming to terms with their moral responsibility, and undergoing spiritual trials and victories. Just as they do in real life.

From England to Narnia and Back Again

During World War II, British cities were subjected to merciless bombing by the Germans. Many parents evacuated their children to the countryside, hoping to prevent them from being killed by Hitler's bombs. As part of his war effort, Lewis signed up for a program to take in evacuees from the city. In 1939, he took in a number of schoolchildren to live for a while at the Kilns, his sprawling old house three miles outside of Oxford.[1] Walter Hooper, Lewis's literary executor, gives more details:

> In the autumn of 1939 four schoolgirls were evacuated from London to Lewis's home on the outskirts of Oxford. It was his adopted "mother," Mrs. Moore, who mainly looked after the evacuees, but Lewis shared the responsibility of entertaining the young visitors. On the back of another book he was writing at the time, I found what I believe to be the germinal passage of the first story of Narnia—*The Lion, the Witch and the Wardrobe*. It says: "This book is about four children whose names were Ann, Martin, Rose and Peter. But it is most about Peter who was the youngest. They all had to go away from London suddenly because of the Air Raids, and because Father, who was in the army, had gone off to the War and Mother was doing some kind of war work. They were sent to stay with a relation of Mother's who was a very old Professor who lived by himself in the country."[2]

So when *The Lion, the Witch and the Wardrobe* opens by saying that the story is about what happened to Lucy, Peter, Susan, and Edmund when they were sent away from London because of the air raids, the story is grounded in the real world. The house with its nooks, crannies, and hiding places sounds very much like the Kilns. And the old Professor, leaving the children to their own devices but understanding them when it counted, is very much like C. S. Lewis.

The fantasy world of Narnia that the children discover through the wardrobe has them encountering unspeakable evil in the form of a witch who seeks to destroy them. We should keep in mind that the story is framed by the real world of twentieth-century Europe, which was also encountering unspeakable evil in the form of Adolf Hitler, who was also seeking to destroy children. Hooper's account underscores World War II—with its bombing of civilians, its disruption of families, and its impact on children—as the context, the inspiration, and the starting point for *The Chronicles of Narnia*.

> Narnia is not the sort of fantasy that is escapist. Lucy, Peter, Susan, and Edmund are not escaping their problems in going to a magical wonderland.

And yet, Narnia is not the sort of fantasy that is escapist. Lucy, Peter, Susan, and Edmund are not escaping their problems in going to a magical wonderland. Narnia is where they face the very same spiritual issues that are operative in their realistic world—and in our real world.

Lucy and Edmund in Narnia

When Lucy finds herself in Narnia, after first exploring inside the wardrobe, she sees Tumnus, the faun with the packages. He is startled when he sees her and asks if she is a Daughter of Eve. He has never seen a girl or any other kind of human being before. As we learn later, being a Son of Adam or a Daughter of Eve conveys on these children a special status in Narnia.

Human beings are lords over the animals. This is true even of talking animals, who are rational enough to acknowledge, as we see later in the story, that the children of Adam and Eve are their rightful kings and queens. This, of course, is a direct reference to the Bible, which specifies that the first couple and their descendants were given "dominion over the fish of the sea and over the birds of the heavens and over every living thing that moves on the earth" (Gen. 1:28). Again, the world of Narnia is reflecting both the truth in Lucy's realistic world (though she has a little trouble realizing what the faun is referring to) and in our real world. In Narnia, though, we can perhaps see this truth more clearly than we are used to doing.

Lucy has a pleasant time with Tumnus, having a tea party in his homey little cave. He plays her some music on his flute. Lucy starts to doze off, but then Tumnus, filled with guilt, starts crying. We learn that Narnia is no paradise—that, as with the paradise of the first Adam and Eve, this wonderful world has fallen into bondage to a devil, who is both tyrant and tempter.

Tumnus confesses that he is employed by someone he calls the White Witch. She has expressly told him to be on guard against any Children of Adam and Eve. If he finds any, he is to catch them and bring them to her. This, in fact, had been his intention in seemingly being so kind to Lucy and inviting her to his house for tea. This is why he has been playing his music, to lull her to sleep. What has seemed so pleasant, we now learn was sinister. But Tumnus has been having a crisis of conscience and, after actually getting to know a human being, he realizes that he can't betray her to the White Witch, even though the costs of defying her can be deadly, to the point of being turned into stone.

Underneath all of these ordinary pleasantries of buttering toast and chitchatting, Tumnus was engaged in a moral struggle, of exactly the kind other characters will go through later. He chose to do what was right, despite the costs. Lucy—and the reader—do not quite realize the magnitude of what he has been saying, so she goes back through the trees (though even they are revealed to be ominous when Tumnus warns her that some of the trees are on the witch's side) to the lamppost, where she sees the door of the wardrobe opening out back into the old house in England.

When she steps out of the wardrobe, she is back to her ordinary life, except that Narnia proves difficult to explain. She had been in Narnia for hours, and yet she steps right back into the moment that she had left, with none of our earth time elapsing. (C. S. Lewis loved science fiction and wrote some classics in the genre. The paradoxes of time—such as the Professor later explaining that the time that takes place in another world might not take up any of the time in our world—are characteristic science-fiction mind teasers.)

Lucy tells her brothers and sister about going to Narnia, but they do not believe her. They check out the wardrobe, but this time, when they move the coats away, it has an ordinary back panel. They assume at first that she is joking, then that she is lying, then that she may have lost her mind.

Edmund is especially vicious about it, teasing and tormenting his little sister. Lucy, in a way that young readers can relate to, is miserable.

A few days later, the children are playing hide-and-seek.

Edmund sees Lucy go into the wardrobe, so he does too, with the intention of giving her a hard time. But as he fumbles around in the wardrobe to find her, Edmund finds himself in Narnia.

What Edmund experiences in Narnia will be discussed in the next chapter. Lucy is overjoyed to find him in Narnia too. Now everyone else will believe her.

> Some sins are twisted and unlawful attempts to gain something good.

But when they return, Edmund, bitter that his sister has been proved right and sulking that he is going to have to admit that he was wrong, betrays her. When Peter and Susan come up to them and when Lucy excitedly says that Edmund has been to Narnia too, Edmund denies it. The two of them have just been playing, he claims, just pretending that there is a Narnia.

Edmund's Sin

The moral degradation of Edmund is one of the story's most important issues. His relationship with the witch, the subject of the next chapter, is a symbol of his sinful condition in this world. There are hints throughout the conversation of the children about how Edmund is at school, implying that he has the kind of bullying, obnoxious personality that makes many of his fellow students—especially those smaller than he is—miserable. What he does to Lucy, though, in betraying her by denying what she says even though he knows it is true, is especially low. He is acting out of "spite," as Peter recognizes.

Some sins are twisted and unlawful attempts to gain something good. A thief who steals a stereo gets to listen to music. A drug addict wrecks his body and his life to get pleasure.

> But there are other sins that give the perpetrator nothing in return.

Those sins are bad enough. But there are other sins that give the perpetrator nothing in return: Vandalism, destroying something just to destroy it. Cruelty, tearing the wings off of an insect or bullying someone weaker than we are just because we can. Pride. Anger. Revenge. Purposefully hurting someone who loves us.

In another of his books, *The Screwtape Letters*, Lewis has a devil exulting when he tempts a person to spiritual destruction and gives nothing in return. In *Mere Christianity*, Lewis distinguishes between "sins of the flesh," involving animal-like pleasures, and sins that are "purely spiritual"—acts of sheer malice, evil for evil's sake, such as hatred, backbiting, putting others in the wrong—which he terms "diabolical."

In Dante's *Inferno*, the lowest circles of hell are for those who have rejected love. Their punishment is the same as the sin they have embraced: With their coldness, they are frozen in ice, alone in their self-chosen isolation. And the very lowest circle of hell is reserved for those who betray those who love them. That was the sin of Judas Iscariot. And that was the sin of Edmund.

But all he did was a little act of childish behavior. It was petty and mean, but surely what a child does while playing hide-and-seek cannot be that important. There was no big, dramatic crime. How could this minor incident be so bad? Everyone does that sort of thing at one time or another. Besides, Edmund is just a little kid.

> *The Lion, the Witch and the Wardrobe* is about sin, and it is about salvation from sin.

Despite the common assumption that children are innocent, children themselves know it is not true. Not only are they commonly victimized by other children's sins—in the schoolyard, in gossipy telephone and computer conversations, in the vicious pecking orders of the juvenile social scene. Children also know that they themselves are subject to these sins, in the way they treat others and in what they know about themselves.

The Lion, the Witch and the Wardrobe is about sin, and it is about salvation from sin. When the setting shifts to Narnia, the moral and spiritual issues are thrown into high relief. But Lewis makes clear from the outset that sin is very ordinary. It does not have to be dramatic, breaking out into some monstrous crime, to be deadly and soul-killing. Sin inheres deeply within our nature. While sin can break out into action, its home is in our thoughts and feelings and attitudes, in the deepest recesses of our heart.

When we read how Edmund acts toward his sister, all of his inner bitterness and self-pitying rationalizations, we can relate to him. No matter how old we are, whether we are adults or Edmund's age, we can identify with him, because his sinfulness is our own.

The Professor and His Logic

Peter and Susan, the two oldest, are worried about Lucy, who keeps insisting there is a Narnia. Even after Edmund denies and ridicules her story, she holds her ground.

Lucy's position will feel familiar to anyone who tries to persuade others about a reality that goes beyond everyday experience. For example, talking about our faith. If we have come to know God in a real and personal way, the whole realm of spiritual truth has opened up to us. We want to talk about it with our friends so that they, too, can know the joy we have found.

And yet, they do not understand. They are so materialistic, so convinced that this world is all there is, that they do not even have a frame of reference for the spiritual realities we are trying to describe. We cannot show them God. We cannot prove the sacrifice of Christ. And yet, we know in the deepest part of our being that these spiritual things are real. But our friends think we are weird. Not only can we not get through to them, to our great frustration and misery, but they may even think we have lost our minds. And it may be that some of them do know that what we are talking about is real, but they deny it in order to get in good with the crowd, just as Edmund did.

Peter and Susan, though sympathetic to Lucy, think there may be something wrong with her, so they decide they had better go to the adult. They approach the Professor in his study and inform him about the wild stories Lucy has been telling.

They are taken aback, though, when he asks them how they know that what she has been saying isn't true.

Peter and Susan are not used to hearing an adult talk that way. They have been assuming that a story about a world in the wardrobe just can't be true. They have been operating out of what their worldview allows them to believe, not out of any evidence or logical train of reasoning.

> Is Jesus Christ who he claimed to be, the incarnate Son of God? There are only three possibilities, he wrote. Either Jesus is a liar, a lunatic, or the Son of God.

Susan does think of some evidence against what Lucy has been saying. She points out to the Professor that Edmund had said the two of them were just pretending.

The Professor concedes the point, but then asks which one, Lucy or Edmund, tends to be more truthful.

Well, that would be Lucy, by far, the two agree.

Then Susan raises another possibility. Maybe Lucy is out of her mind. The Professor replies that all Susan and Peter have to do is talk with Lucy and they can tell that she isn't mad.

Then the Professor goes off on a mini-rant about how schools don't teach logic anymore. There are only three possibilities, he says. Either Lucy is lying, or she is insane, or she is telling the truth.

Those who know Lucy know that she is not a liar and that she is not insane. Therefore, concludes the Professor, unless more evidence comes up, the logical conclusion is that she must be telling the truth.

We will learn more about this particular Professor—and his wardrobe—in *The Magician's Nephew*.[3] But this exchange, which continues along these lines, is directly reminiscent of a famous argument made by the real Professor who took war-refugee children into his home, Professor C. S. Lewis.

In his book *Mere Christianity*, Lewis applies this very same logic to the claims of Christ. Is Jesus Christ who he claimed to be, the incarnate Son of God? There are only three possibilities, he wrote. Either Jesus is a liar, a lunatic, or the Son of God.[4]

From what we know of him in all of the accounts of his life, Jesus embodied the highest virtues. It is hard to believe that someone who did the things he did would be a liar. By the same token, his personality is not that of a madman, someone who believes he is a poached egg. Rather, the words and wisdom of Jesus are profoundly sane. Therefore, Jesus must be the Son of God, and we should fall at his feet in adoration.

That argument has cut through the defenses of thousands of readers. It has been cited by many as helping them realize who Jesus is and as being instrumental in bringing them to faith.

Not that Lucy is a stand-in for Christ, or Narnia for heaven. But both in his nonfiction apologetics and in his radically fictional fantasy novels, Lewis is demonstrating how to think. He is showing that it is possible for Christians to use both their mind and their imagination, and that the two can work together hand in hand.

It is possible to think clearly and objectively about truths that lie beyond what we can physically perceive. While this does not mean that we can necessarily be reasoned into faith, since faith is a gift of God and not a matter of mere intellectual knowledge, there is a place for the Christian mind, both in its capacities of reason and of imagination. These two are often considered opposites today, but only because the contemporary mind has artificially split them apart, not knowing the creator who gives them unity. Good thinking should not lead us away from the Christian worldview, but it can take us, as Lewis says elsewhere in *The Chronicles of Narnia*, further up and farther in.

CHAPTER 3

THE WHITE WITCH

The Reign of the Devil

Some Christians refuse to have anything to do with *The Lion, the Witch and the Wardrobe* because the title has the word "Witch" in it. They assume, therefore, that the story has to do with the occult. In some versions of the objection, the word "Witch" can be an entry point for demonic powers. Some parents have gone on a crusade to get the book out of schools and off classroom reading lists—which is ironic, since, as we will see, there can hardly be a more Christian and gospel-proclaiming novel.

Most Christians are pleased when this explicitly Christian literary classic makes its way into a school's curriculum. Usually, it would be the other side, those who do not want children or anyone else exposed to Christianity—who would want this book out of the schools. But maybe they likewise see the word "Witch" in the title and jump to the same conclusion, agreeing that any book with "Witch" in the title must be occult, but thinking that is a good reason to have it in the curriculum.

> The story explores in symbol what the Bible says about Satan's reign in a fallen world.

Neither side is paying attention to what the witch and the book as a whole *mean*. This comes down to knowing how to read. Simply knowing that a story has a witch in it tells us nothing about what it says about the witch: Is the witch the heroine? Or the villain? Does the story make us want to be like the witch? Or does the story make us reject witchcraft and all that it stands for?

In *The Lion, the Witch and the Wardrobe,* the witch symbolizes Satan. The story explores in symbol what the Bible says about Satan's reign in a fallen world; how he tempts us; how he enslaves us; and how he is defeated by Jesus Christ, who frees us from his bondage.

Always Winter and Never Christmas

We first learn about the White Witch when Lucy is having her pleasant tea with Tumnus. She drifts off due to the music he plays for her, but she comes to herself when her host starts crying and wailing. When she asks why he is so upset, he confesses that he is a bad faun, the worst faun there has ever been. Lucy tries to console him. She insists that he is the nicest faun she has ever met—though, of course, he is the *only* faun she has ever met. How could this kindly, jovial creature be a bad person, she wonders.

But he is. Tumnus admits that he is in the service of the

White Witch. He works for her. She pays him. His job is to guard the borders of Narnia and to watch for any Sons of Adam or Daughters of Eve. If he finds any, he is to capture them—his method is to lull them to sleep, and turn them over to the White Witch.

Tumnus still has a conscience, though; and when he sees how likeable this Daughter of Eve actually is—apparently in contradiction to the witch's propaganda—he cannot go through with his plan to capture her. His hospitality, we learn, while it appeared kindly, was actually, at first, a trap to lure Lucy to her doom. But he is guilt-ridden for having deceived her. He confesses his sin and repents. Tumnus, at great risk to his life, disobeys the witch and resolves instead to protect Lucy.

When Lucy asks him who the White Witch is, Tumnus tells her that she is the one who has all Narnia "under her thumb." (For more on the origins of the witch, follow this end note.[1]) Because of her, it is always winter. And it is never Christmas.

Those simple words are charged with symbolism. In the later story, *The Magician's Nephew*, we learn the details of the creation of Narnia but also of its fall. We learn who the witch is and how she got into Narnia. Without spoiling the story for those who have not yet read it, suffice it to say that the fall of Narnia and the reign of the witch came about because of a Son of

> As in that real world that we inhabit, Narnia is under a curse. It is always winter.

Adam. Human sinfulness from the fallen real world has been exported into the new world of Narnia.

As in that real world that we inhabit, Narnia is under a curse. It is always winter. It is cold, frozen. In our world, winter is a time when the plants and trees become lifeless. Though a spark of life does remain, blooming in the resurrection of spring, winter signifies a time of death.

There is one good thing about winter though—Christmas. The fact that the most joyful holiday of the year takes place in the depressing depths of winter is symbolic in itself. The light of Christ comes precisely in our moment of greatest darkness (John 1:4–5). In winter we find a time of hope.

But Narnia, under the thumb of the White Witch, is a world in which Christ has not yet come. And because Christ has not come, there is no Christmas—just winter all the time, under the cold-hearted reign of the Evil One.

The Beautiful Queen of Narnia

When Edmund first goes into Narnia, he, being evil himself, runs right into the White Witch. When he sees her, swathed in white furs, riding on her sleigh, he is struck by how beautiful she is.

This is important to remember about the manifestations of Satan. Once again we have presented to us the conflict between appearance and reality. Satan and the witch in reality are hideously monstrous in their true inner selves, but they *appear* attractive, persuasive, and good. "Satan disguises himself as an angel of light" (2 Cor. 11:14). And so do those who serve him. "So it is no surprise if his servants, also, disguise themselves as servants of righteousness" (v. 15).

Evil generally presents itself as something *good*. We seldom are tempted by someone saying, "Let's do something evil today." Rather, our temptations come in the guise of virtues. Sexual immorality masquerades as love. Cruelty pretends to be justice. Rebellion insists that it is freedom.

Our desires for relationships, laudable in themselves, often lead us into sin, as we do things we would not otherwise do in order to be liked and accepted by our friends. The Devil literally appears as an angel of light in the way he founds false religions—often accompanied by visions of "angels"—that seem oh-so-mystical and meaningful.

So, of course, the White Witch is beautiful. Even when he first meets her, however, Edmund notes that she is also "proud and cold and stern" (p. 27). The Devil does not love us. For all of the fun and frolic, the love and the freedom that *seem* to be promised by the various angels of light that allure us, the Devil actually gives us misery, hatred, and bondage.

The White Witch introduces herself to Edmund as the Queen of Narnia. Lucy later says that she only calls herself the queen. She is not really queen by right. Satan is sometimes called "the ruler of this world" (John 12:31), and so he is, by conquest but not by right. Christ is the true King, the "only Sovereign, the King of kings and Lord of lords" (1 Tim. 6:15). The Devil—

> The White Witch can turn living things into stone.

with the witch—is a usurper: not the creator, not the source of all authority, not the providential governor of all things, but a rebellious, spiteful egotist, a tyrannical dictator who rules by force for his own aggrandizement.

The Devil—as with the witch—is powerful and dangerous though. As Tumnus tells Lucy, the White Witch can turn living things into stone. The author of the book of Hebrews says that Christians should exhort each other, "that none of you may be hardened by the deceitfulness of sin" (Heb. 3:13). "Do not harden your hearts as in the rebellion" (v. 15). Scripture describes how sin *hardens* people, making them *less* sensitive, *less* feeling, and *less* responsive to God and to each other.

> Sin *hardens* people, making them *less* sensitive, *less* feeling, and *less* responsive to God and to each other.

The apostle Paul talks about those whose "consciences are seared" (1 Tim. 4:2). In the first chapter of Romans, he describes the history of sin, both in mankind as a whole and, as many will recognize, in the life of an individual, how sin gets worse and worse as it is given free rein. This hardening is vividly described by the prophet Ezekiel, who characterizes those who reject God as having a "heart of stone" (Ezek. 11:19).

Turkish Delight

When Edmund is first confronted by the White Witch, he is scared. Demanding that he cower before "the Queen of Narnia," she learns that he is a Son of Adam. This is of great concern to her because, in the creation of the universe, Adam and his descendants were given sovereignty over the animals. At that time God said:

> "Let us make man in our image, after our likeness. And let them have dominion over the fish of the sea and over the birds of the heavens and over the livestock and over all the earth and over every creeping thing that creeps on the earth." (Gen. 1:26)

That means that in Narnia, a world of talking animals, the rightful ruler must be a Son of Adam. The usurping queen, the witch, has set guards like Tumnus to be on the lookout for any Son of Adam or Daughter of Eve, since any human being would be a direct threat to her reign.

The White Witch muses that this one descendant of Adam is easily taken care of, and she raises her wand to destroy Edmund; but she suddenly stops and gets a better idea. All of a sudden, she turns nice. She gets all cutesy with him, calling him a poor child, inviting him onto her sleigh, wrapping her fur mantle around him.

She conjures up something hot to drink, something pleasant that he has never tasted before. Then she asks him what his favorite food is. Turkish Delight, he tells her.

At one point, doing research on C. S. Lewis, I scoured the ethnic neighborhoods of Chicago in an effort to actually find some Turkish Delight, to see if it was everything Edmund cracked it up to be. I finally found some in a Greek food store.

Turkish Delight is a candy, something like a gumdrop—a gooey, gelatinous confection rolled in sugar. It comes in different colors and flavors. What I tasted was sickeningly sweet.

Edmund, though, loves that kind of decadent treat, and

the White Witch gives him the best Turkish Delight he has ever tasted. He devours it as the witch interrogates him about his background and about his brother and sisters. She knows that there are four thrones at the castle of Cair Paravel, and she knows the prophecies about four human beings who will one day rule in Narnia. Like Herod, she resolves to find and kill these potential rivals to her rule.

As Edmund is gorging himself on sticky candy, he "spills his guts" to the false queen, telling her everything she wants to know, including how Lucy has already been there and how she has met a faun. When the Turkish Delight runs out, Edmund wants some more, but the witch does not give him any. Instead, she asks him to bring Peter, Lucy, and Susan to her. If he does, she will give him some more Turkish Delight.

One characteristic of an addiction is that as the craving grows, the actual pleasure grows less, requiring more and more stimulation to achieve the desired effect.

Edmund craves the witch's Turkish Delight and will do anything to get more. What he does not realize is that what the witch has given him is enchanted. Those who taste it once will want more and more. If they could get enough, they would eat it and eat it until they killed themselves.

Sinful pleasures are like that. Edmund becomes addicted to the witch's Turkish Delight. Similarly, drug addicts develop such cravings that they will lie, steal, and even kill in order to get another hit of drugs. A drug addict will even keep taking drugs until they kill him. The one addictive pleasure leads to more and more sins. Alcohol can have the same effect. Sexual sins can be similarly addictive and destructive.

One characteristic of an addiction is that as the craving grows, the actual pleasure grows less, requiring more and more stimulation to achieve the desired effect. This is why drug addicts require greater and greater amounts of the drug, to the point of death by overdose. Alcoholics drink more and more, despite what it does to their families and to their own lives. The sexual titillation from pornography has to keep getting more and more extreme or the thrill will be gone, leading to ever more extreme perversions, from kiddy porn to acting out those fantasies in fornication, child molestation, and rape.

But less dramatic sins also have the quality of Turkish Delight. We can gorge ourselves on hatred, as well, or on envy or greed or pride. All of these are egotistical pleasures, which we come to crave and which lead to other, more overt sins.

Turkish Delight also symbolizes the sense in which sin is enslaving. Drug addicts, alcoholics, and sexual obsessives are not free. Their bondage may start with an exhilarating sense of freedom, of rebellion against the norm, of an exciting exercise of personal choice. But these sins make those who indulge in them slaves. Addicts cannot just choose to stop their habits. If they were free, they could. Even when they *want* to stop, they cannot, as their desires drag them deeper and deeper into self-destruction.

And all sin is like that. Contrary to the popular assumption that sin is liberating, the truth is that sin destroys freedom. Sin leads to bondage. As Jesus himself said, "Everyone who commits sin is a slave to sin" (John 8:34). (He also said, "If the Son sets you free, you will be free indeed" [v. 36].)

The witch soon plies Edmund with more than enchanted candy. She appeals to his ego and resentments as well. "If you bring your brother and sisters to me," she tells him, "we will all go to my house. There, not only will you have all the Turkish Delight you want, I will make you my prince. Someday you will get to be king. And you can rule over Peter and Lucy and Susan."

The point of the Turkish Delight is that Edmund is now in bondage to the witch, just as real sinners are in bondage to Satan.

Which Is the Right Side?

Back in our world, Edmund's sinfulness manifests itself in a petty, childish act of betrayal. As discussed in the last chapter, he denies that there is a Narnia, even after being there, just to torment his sister Lucy.

One day, some tourists are getting a tour through the old house. To avoid them, all four of the children dash into the wardrobe to hide. Now, they all find themselves in Narnia. Peter and Susan realize that Lucy has been telling the truth all along. They apologize. But they also realize that Edmund has been lying and has betrayed Lucy. Peter calls him a "poisonous little beast" (p. 53).

And like other sinners caught in the act, instead of repenting, Edmund responds to his exposure with resentment and a desire to strike out at his accusers. "All of you little stuck-up brats," he thinks; "I'll pay you back for this."

With Lucy in the lead, they head off for Tumnus's house.

But instead of the cozy, hospitable place Lucy remembers, they find the door broken down and the place ransacked. The dishes have been smashed. The pictures have been slashed. A notice has been nailed to the floor, announcing that Tumnus has been arrested for treason and for fraternizing with humans, the queen's enemies. Underscoring the totalitarian nature of the queen's rule—and that of Satan—the proclamation is signed by a wolf, a captain of the witch's secret police.

This, too, is Edmund's fault. He told the witch about the faun's meeting with Lucy. Tumnus refused to betray her to the witch, and now he is paying the penalty. He has sacrificed himself for the Daughter of Eve.

Now the children experience an overwhelming sense of responsibility. "It isn't safe here," Susan observes. "Let's just go back."

"But we can't do that," says Lucy. "Tumnus got into trouble with the witch because of me. We have to find a way to rescue him." Susan says she wishes they had never come, but she agrees that since they are here, they have a responsibility to Tumnus. Peter agrees, but how can they even know where to look for Tumnus?

A robin starts hopping around. They get the impression that the bird wants them to follow him, so they do.

Edmund sidles up to Peter and asks how he knows what side the robin is on. The bird may be leading them into a trap. Peter, though, drawing on the wisdom of his traditional education, says that robins are the good guys in all of the stories he has read.

But Edmund goes further. "How do we know the faun was on the right side? How do we know the queen is really a witch? How do we know she is on the wrong side? Who are

> Edmund has taken the next step in his degradation. His moral failures are corrupting his thinking.

we to say who is right and who is wrong?"

Edmund has taken the next step in his degradation. His moral failures are corrupting his thinking. The moral decline chronicled in Romans 1 is accompanied by the "debased mind" (v. 28) in which sinners "by their unrighteousness suppress the truth" (v. 18). Rationalizations, excuses, the construction of false philosophies and idolatrous religions are all ways of evading God and of approving sin (v. 32). Edmund, like a postmodernist, is questioning whether there even are objective standards of right and wrong. Edmund has become a relativist.

CHAPTER 4

ASLAN

The Lion of Judah

The robin leads the children to a beaver hiding in the woods—a talking beaver, in resistance to the White Witch. He takes them past his dam to his house, a beaver lodge made of sticks that is also a warm, cozy cottage. The whole scene, with Mrs. Beaver at her sewing machine and Mr. Beaver frying up some fish, is reminiscent of Beatrix Potter, whose ability in books like *The Adventures of Peter Rabbit* to make her characters both animal-like and human-like, Lewis greatly admired.[1]

As the children tell him about their problems—about poor Tumnus, who contacted Mr. Beaver before his arrest while trying desperately to figure out what to do—Mr. Beaver whispers that "Aslan is on the move."

When they hear this name, each of the children feels something stir inside. Though they do not know who Aslan is, Peter feels brave and intrepid; Susan feels as if she has just smelled something delicious or heard beautiful music;

Lucy feels like the holidays or the first days of summer have begun; Edmund feels a stab of horror. This name brings out each child's nature. The other children respond to Aslan with joy, but Edmund, the sinner, draws back in fear.

> It is Aslan who must do the saving.

They ask who Aslan is and are told that he is the King of the Wood, the Son of the great Emperor-Beyond-the-Sea. He is the King of Beasts, the great lion, whose coming—according to the prophecies—will make spring come again.

The children try to plan some "strategem" to rescue Tumnus, dressing up in disguises and other elaborate schemes such as they have read about in their books. But their works will be futile against the witch, Mr. Beaver tells them. It is Aslan who must do the saving.

The Lion of Judah

The figure of Aslan is the soul of all *The Chronicles of Narnia*. With Aslan, the fantasy becomes an allegory. Aslan is the center of the stories' meaning and the main source of their insight. Aslan, of course, is Lewis's symbol for Jesus Christ.[2]

In the real world, according to the doctrine of the incarnation, God became man in Jesus Christ. The second person of the Trinity entered his creation, taking on our human flesh and our human nature, in order to save us.

> In the beginning was the Word, and the Word was with
> God, and the Word was God. He was in the beginning
> with God. All things were made through him, and with-
> out him was not any thing made that was made. In him
> was life, and the life was the light of men.... And the
> Word became flesh and dwelt among us. (John 1:1–4, 14)

In terms of Lewis's imaginary sub-creation, Narnia is another world. It is populated by talking animals. Just as the Son of God became a human being to save a world of human beings, so he becomes a talking animal to save a world of talking animals. In a letter to a friend, Lewis explained that Aslan "is an invention giving an imaginary answer to the question, 'What might Christ become like, if

> ### Aslan, throughout the series, demonstrates his "true Beasthood."

there really were a world like Narnia and he chose to be incarnate and die and rise again in that world as he actually has done in ours?'"[3]

Kathryn Lindskoog explains the idea by quoting what she calls "a capricious bit of speculation" from Lewis's contemporary and fellow apologist, Dorothy L. Sayers:

> It was said, sneeringly, by someone that if a clam
> could conceive of God, it would conceive of him in
> the shape of a great, big clam. Naturally. And if God
> has revealed himself to clams, it could be only under
> conditions of perfect clamhood, since any other
> manifestation would be wholly irrelevant to clam
> nature. By incarnation, the creator says in effect:
> "See! This is what my eternal Idea looks like in terms

of my own creation; this is my manhood, this is my clamhood, this is my characterhood in a volume of created characters."[4]

Thus, just as Jesus Christ is true man and true God, in the world of talking beasts Aslan, throughout the series, demonstrates what Lindskoog calls his "true Beasthood,"[5] purring like a big cat, lashing his tail, letting the children stroke his mane.

Of course, all of this is a fictional construct. God did not become incarnate as a clam to clams—the Bible tells us that his incarnation as a human being of flesh and blood and his saving work are sufficient to redeem the whole physical creation, which would presumably include clams as well (Rom. 8:19–23). And Narnia exists only in the imagination of both its author and its readers. But Lewis is nevertheless modeling his lion on what he knows of Jesus Christ, who is thus Lewis's source for the character, just as other details in the books have as their source real-world truths. So although *The Chronicles of Narnia* are not allegorical, as such, they still contain images that resonate with meaning for our world, which is their ultimate source. Clyde Kilby calls them not allegories but "analogies."[6] At any rate, Lewis's fictional world is written so as to be *symbolic* of truths in the real world. And Aslan is a *symbol* of Christ.

The word "Aslan" is simply the Persian word for lion. The Bible itself uses the lion as a symbol for Christ.

One of the earliest prophecies of the coming of Christ given in Scripture uses the symbol of the lion. Jacob, on his deathbed, gives a blessing to each of his twelve sons, who will become the patriarchs who father the twelve tribes of Israel. When he comes to Judah, in whose line will come the royal house of David and Jesus Christ himself, Jacob, speaking as a prophet by inspiration of the Holy Spirit, says this:

> Judah is a lion's cub;
>> from the prey, my son, you have gone up.
> He stooped down; he crouched as a lion
>> and as a lioness; who dares rouse him?
> The scepter shall not depart from Judah,
>> nor the ruler's staff from between his feet,
> until tribute comes to him;
>> and to him shall be the obedience of the peoples.
> Binding his foal to the vine
>> and his donkey's colt to the choice vine,
> he has washed his garments in wine
>> and his vesture in the blood of grapes.
> (Gen. 49:9–11)

These words seem mysterious and enigmatic. But their imagery recalls immediately from the life of Christ: the donkey's foal he rode on in his triumphal entry; the vine; wine as blood, as in Holy Communion; and his garments drenched in sacramental blood, as in his Passion. The words could not be clearer as a prophecy that Judah's line will produce the king, with his scepter and ruler's staff. But the prediction goes beyond the coming of David and his dynasty. The scepter will never depart from Judah. This speaks of an eternal kingdom. All of the peoples will pay tribute and owe obedience to this King.

But what does the lion have to do with it? Judah is described as a cub, a baby lion. He acts lion-like in that he is crouching, as if about to charge. This lion is poised to attack, so that it is dangerous to "rouse him." But the imagery is all about the *potential* of Jacob's lionhood. The baby lion getting ready to charge points to the prophecy's fulfillment in the future, in the coming of David and in the coming of Christ.

The lion has become associated with kingship in nearly every culture. When Solomon succeeded his father David, in fulfillment of Jacob's prophecy, he built "a great ivory throne" inlaid with gold with "two lions standing beside the armrests, while twelve lions stood there, one on each end of a step on the six steps" (1 Kings 10:18–20). Solomon's scepter, his ruling staff between his feet, would have been set off by images of lions.

> Lions, though, are also awe-inspiring. Their strength, their dignity, their ferocity fill us with wonder and admiration.

Lions also appeared in the temple itself. Lest anyone worry that a lion image might be some kind of idol, God himself called for carvings of lions—along with cherubim, oxen, and palm trees—to adorn the stands to be used in the temple to hold the basins for cleansing water (1 Kings 7:29, 36), the typology pointing forward to Christian baptism.

Now a symbol can have more than one meaning, depending upon what aspects are being emphasized. Certainly, a lion is a dangerous animal. Both Samson and David had to fight lions. David used the figure of a ravenous lion ripping its prey apart as a way to describe the hatred of his enemies (Ps. 7:1–2). In the New Testament, Peter uses a man-eating lion to describe Satan: "Your adversary the devil prowls around like a roaring lion, seeking someone to devour" (1 Peter 5:8).

Lions, though, are also awe-inspiring. Their strength, their dignity, their ferocity fill us with wonder and admiration. These qualities are "kingly." The animal itself evokes feelings that make it a worthy symbol for authority and majesty.

Scripture also uses the lion as a symbol of God's people. The prophet Balaam is hired to curse the children of Israel, but instead he blesses them and compares them to lions:

> Behold a people! As a lioness it rises up
>   and as a lion it lifts itself;
> it does not lie down until it has devoured the prey
>   and drunk the blood of the slain. (Num. 23:24)

This refers to the military power of the Israelites as they defeat the peoples of the land that God has given them.

This violence of the lion is also ascribed to God himself, as he comes in judgment:

> For thus the LORD said to me,
> "As a lion or a young lion growls over his prey,
>   and when a band of shepherds is called out
>   against him
> is not terrified by their shouting
>   or daunted at their noise,
> so the LORD of hosts will come down
>   to fight on Mount Zion and on its hill." (Isa. 31:4)

This figure of God's judgment as being like the attack of a lion is repeated often by the prophets (e.g., Jer. 4:7–8; Hos. 13:4–9).

But sometimes the lion of God's judgment undergoes a transformation:

> For I will be like a lion to Ephraim,
>> and like a young lion to the house of Judah.
> I, even I, will tear and go away;
>> I will carry off, and no one shall rescue.
> I will return again to my place,
>> until they acknowledge their guilt and seek my face,
>> and in their distress earnestly seek me.
> "Come, let us return to the LORD;
>> for he has torn us, that he may heal us;
>> he has struck us down, and he will bind us up.
> After two days he will revive us;
>> on the third day he will raise us up,
>> that we may live before him." (Hos. 5:14–6:2)

Here is judgment that leads to repentance and salvation. The lion that has torn now heals. He has struck, but now he binds up. Those who acknowledge their guilt and seek the Lord's face will be forgiven. The condemnation of the Law provokes repentance and transforms into the forgiveness of the gospel. This passage includes a remarkable prophecy of the resurrection, of Christ's and of our own in his (Rom. 6:3–11).

The most explicit portrayal of Christ as the Lion of Judah is in the book of Revelation:

> Behold, the Lion of the tribe of Judah, the Root of David, has conquered, so that he can open the scroll and its seven seals. (Rev. 5:5)

But when the writer of these words looks at the Lion, what he sees is a Lamb. The Lamb is the one who opens the scroll and the seven seals. The Lion and the Lamb are the same person. He receives the praise of the saints and of "myriads of myriads and thousands of thousands" of angels, singing,

> Worthy are you to take the scroll and to open its
>   seals,
> for you were slain, and by your blood you ransomed
>   people for God
>   from every tribe and language and people and
>   nation,
> and you have made them a kingdom and priests to
>   our God,
>   and they shall reign on the earth.
> Worthy is the Lam who was slain, to receive power
> and wealth and wisdom and might and honor and
> glory and blessing. (Rev. 5:9–10, 12)

In other words, the Lion has become the Lamb who gave himself as a sacrifice to atone for the sins of the world, ransoming the saints with his blood.

Not a Tame Lion

When Mr. Beaver tells the children that they are to meet Aslan at the Stone Table, Susan is leery of the prospect of facing a lion. She asks if he is safe.

> Today, we have domesticated God.

"No," Mr. Beaver tells her. "He is not safe. But he is good."

Today, we have domesticated God. People tend to imagine him as a kindly old man with a white beard. (Note that such a human picture of God is no less figurative and symbolic than Lewis's lion.[7]) "The God that I believe in," they say, "would never punish anyone." They assume that because God is benevolent and loving, he must be *nice*.

Jesus, in particular, has been sentimentalized. "Gentle Jesus, meek and mild" has become a stereotype. Paintings and illustrations of our Lord in devotional art portray him as feminized, almost androgynous. He has come to be thought of as so soft and benign that, to many people, he has become nonthreatening, someone they can mold to their own desires (as we see in much liberal theology, or even the presumptuous habit non-Christians have of trying to make Jesus one of their own). It is true that Jesus is gentle, meek, and mild; but he is also the man who threw out the money-changers, who castigated the Pharisees as whitewashed tombs, who will gird on his sword and come again in glory to overthrow the Antichrist and the Beast and to judge the living and the dead.

To portray Jesus correctly and effectively—whether in a painting, a book, or a sermon—is very difficult.[8] He is both God and man. Some works communicate his divinity, as in the imposing Byzantine mosaics of Christ Pantokrator, showing Jesus sternly judging the world. And yet, these miss his humanity, as well as his grace. Other paintings show his humanity—Jesus as a cute little baby—but miss his divinity. In the best religious art, the work—while perhaps its subject matter emphasizes one or the other—conveys both. The cute baby Jesus holds on to his mother, stressing his humanity, but he also seems to be looking at us with an expression beyond his years, reaching out to us, signing a blessing, as a thornbush and a lamb in the background remind us that he has come to die for us.

The other paradox, again, is that he is both Lord and

Savior, our Judge and our Advocate. As the scriptural imagery conveys so well, he is both Lion and Lamb.

But what has been most lost in our conception of God today is his *holiness*. God is *different* from us. He is "other." He is set apart. More than that, as is said specifically of the Christ to come, he is "high and lifted up" (Isa. 52:13).

As John Kleinig has noted, God's holiness has to do with his power, his nature, what makes him— and him alone—God, though other things can become holy by contact with him (the Holy Bible, being the Word of God; we become holy—sanctified— through our connection to Christ).⁹

> God's holiness means that he is dangerous. He is not safe. But his holiness also means that he is good. He is, indeed, loving; but he changes lives.

God's holiness also means that he is a "consuming fire" (Heb. 12:29). Sinners cannot stand before a holy God. They would be consumed like the sons of Aaron (Lev. 10:1–3) or Uzzah (2 Sam. 6:5–7), who violated God's holiness. This is why we must have a sinless Mediator who covers us in his sacrificial blood, in whom we can have free access to the throne of God (Heb. 8–9). We can now worship him in "reverence and awe" (Heb. 12:28).

The point is that God's holiness means that he is dangerous. He is not safe. But his holiness also means that he is good. He is, indeed, loving; but he changes lives.

God is also sovereign. That is to say, he is free, and because he is all-powerful, his freedom is unlimited. He does what he pleases. We cannot understand his ways (Rom. 11:33–34). His Holy Spirit is like the wind that "blows where it wishes" (John 3:8). If we may say so, God is wild.

Similarly, as Mr. Beaver explains, Aslan is not a tame lion.

The Coming of Christmas

With Aslan, Lewis is communicating qualities of God by the figure of a majestic lion.[10] Another modern writer, T. S. Eliot, who also converted to Christianity from unbelief, does something similar in his poem "Gerontion":

> ... In the juvescence of the year
> Came Christ the tiger
> In depraved May, dogwood and chestnut, flowering
>   judas,
> To be eaten, to be divided, to be drunk
> Among whispers....
> . . . .
> The tiger springs in the new year. Us he devours.
>   Think at last
> We have not reached conclusion, when I
> Stiffen in a rented house. (ll. 19–23, 49–51)[11]

To Eliot, Christ is like a tiger, lurking in the corners of his life until he finally "springs." Christ the tiger devours us, destroying our old lives and taking us into himself. Eliot's descriptions of the ferocity of Christ are interspersed with references to his sacrifice. The "flowering judas" is a plant, but the name reminds us of Christ's betrayer and thus his passion. Eliot then alludes to the Last Supper and thus to Holy Communion

("Take, eat; this is my body.... Drink of it, all of you, for this is my blood of the covenant, which is poured out for many for the forgiveness of sins" [Matt. 26:26–28].) The tiger, though, is full of life and vitality, in contrast to the speaker of the poem. The title, "Gerontion," means old man, one who will die, stiffening in the rented house of his physical body. But, thanks to Christ the tiger, that will not be his "conclusion."

All of this happens in the spring, the "juvescence" or the young days of the year, in May, which might be called "depraved" for all of the mating that goes on in the animal world. For Eliot, spring, the season of the year when the plants awaken from their winter death, is a symbol of new life.

Lewis paints the same picture in *The Lion, the Witch and the Wardrobe*. As Mr. Beaver and the children head to the Stone Table for their rendezvous with Aslan, and as the White Witch rides her sleigh to intercept them, the snow begins to melt. Patches of green grass can be seen. The witch's sleigh keeps getting bogged down. It is getting warmer. Spring is coming. Because Aslan is coming.

Under the witch, it is always winter, but never Christmas. The coming of Aslan means the breaking of the spell. Now, not only is winter passing, Christmas finally arrives!

> The Father Christmas scene has an important symbolic function: It relates Christmas to the coming of Aslan.

This event is signaled in the book when the children and the beaver run into Father Christmas—the British equivalent of Santa Claus. The witch, he says, has kept him away a long time, but he has finally broken through, thanks to Aslan's being on the move. He gives the children grown-up, "serious kinds" of presents that will be important to their work in Narnia: Peter gets a sword and shield; Susan gets a bow, a quiver of arrows, and a horn; Lucy gets a dagger and a vial of healing elixir. Father Christmas rides off with a "Merry Christmas!" and "Long live the true King!"

> The figure of Aslan in the fantasy world stands for Christ in the real world.

A number of critics do not like this scene. They say that it mixes a legend from our world into Narnia, thus violating the self-contained fantasy world. Father Christmas generally gets cut out of dramatic productions of the story.

The Father Christmas scene has an important symbolic function: It relates Christmas to the coming of Aslan. Therefore, it underscores Lewis's meaning, lest there be any doubt. The figure of Aslan in the fantasy world stands for Christ in the real world.

And when the children arrive at the Stone Table, they do meet Aslan. They are awestruck, yet joyful. But Aslan's work is still to be done.

Is Aslan an Idol?

Some Christians worry about Lewis's depiction of Christ as a great lion. Could that be idolatry? Again, as we have seen, the lion is a *biblical* symbol for Christ, so there cannot be anything intrinsically wrong with employing that symbol in a story.

Still, some people are concerned lest their imaginative conception of God lead them astray. Augustine struggled with this issue in the time of the early church:

> Though I thought not of Thee under the form of a human body, yet was I constrained to image Thee to be something corporeal in space, either infused into the world, or infinitely diffused beyond it ... since whatsoever I conceived, deprived of this space, appeared as nothing to me, yea, altogether nothing, not even a void.[12]

The problem is that even a vague something "infused" or "diffused" through space is a mental image. So is a "void." Lewis memorably addressed the problem in his book *Miracles*:

> "I don't believe in a personal God," says one, "but I do believe in a great spiritual force." What he has not noticed is that the word "force" has let in all sorts of images about winds and tides and electricity and gravitation. "I don't believe in a personal God," says another, "but I do believe we all are parts of one great Being which moves and works through us all"—not noticing that he has merely exchanged the image of a fatherly and royal-looking man for the image of some widely extended gas or fluid. A girl I knew was brought up by "higher thinking" parents to regard God as a perfect "substance"; in later life she realized that this had actually led her to think of him as something like a vast tapioca pudding. (To make matters worse, she disliked tapioca).[13]

Martin Luther, writing at the height of the iconoclastic controversy—trying to calm down his followers who were burning altars and smashing stained-glass windows—insisted that, first of all, the commandment forbidding graven images cannot apply to *mental* images, which we simply cannot avoid, since for us to think of anything involves the automatic functioning of our imagination. The commandment has to do with *graven* images—that is, works carved out of stone or other physical material—that are used as gods, worshipped and venerated as alternatives to the true God who is spirit and truth (John 4:24). Luther went on to argue that because mental images are not prohibited, artistic images are allowed also, thus being one of the first to link art to the imagination. His point was that there can be a non-idolatrous approach to art, even to religious art, even to art that is emblematic of the true God.[14]

We are delivered from these conundrums caused by our mental apparatus by God himself. He reveals himself to us in tangible, even sensory terms, so that we can fully know him.

> That which was from the beginning, which we have heard, which we have seen with our eyes, which we looked upon and have touched with our hands, concerning the word of life—the life was made manifest, and we have seen it, and testify to it and proclaim to you the eternal life, which was with the Father and was made manifest to us. (1 John 1:1–2)

John is referring to the Word made flesh (John 1:14 KJV). God became incarnate in Jesus Christ so that, while we are certainly unable to see the Father directly, we can see him through his Son, as Jesus himself testified: "Whoever sees me sees him who sent me" (John 12:45).

The incarnate Son of God, in turn, gives us other tangible, physical means of knowing him. He uses the water of baptism. He uses bread and wine to commune with us. He gives us his Word—sound waves in the air; ink marks on paper bound into a book—to speak to us directly.

So the problem of our mental images of God—how we should picture him—is resolved. When we think of God, we should think of Jesus Christ. But how should we imagine *him*, not knowing what he looks like? He is the Word made flesh. That means we should imagine God in a way informed by his Word. The particular picture we have in mind is not so important, and should probably change as the different biblical attributes of God come to our minds—our Good Shepherd, our heavenly Father, our righteous Judge, Jesus bleeding in agony on the cross.

> The images and concepts that God gives us to think about him reveal the true God, not false gods.

Insofar as our imagination is shaped and formed by God's Word, we do not have to worry about mental idolatry, since the images and concepts that God gives us to think about him reveal the true God, not false gods. And I would argue that the figure of Aslan is—as I hope I have shown—a figurative representation of Christ that has been shaped and determined by the Word of God.

But some Christians still worry, lest they or their children in their devotional lives substitute thoughts of this lion—so numinous, so compelling—for Jesus. One nine-year-old reader named Laurence worried that he was coming to love Aslan more than he loved Jesus. His mother wrote Lewis, who came back with a sensitive reply:

> But Laurence can't really love Aslan more than Jesus, even if he feels that's what he is doing. For the things he loves Aslan for doing or saying are simply the things Jesus really did and said. So that when Laurence thinks he is loving Aslan, he is really loving Jesus: and perhaps loving him more than he ever did before. Of course there is one thing Aslan has that Jesus has not—I mean, the body of a lion.... Now if Laurence is bothered because he finds the lion-body seems nicer to him than the man-body, I don't think he need be bothered at all. God knows all about the way a little boy's imagination works (he made it, after all) and knows that at a certain age the idea of talking and friendly animals is very attractive. So I don't think he minds if Laurence likes the lion-body. And anyway, Laurence will find as he grows older, that feeling (liking the lion-body better) will die away of itself, without his taking any trouble about it. So he needn't bother.[15]

He went on to recommend that Laurence pray to God, asking him to remove those thoughts and feelings if they are bad, and, if they are not bad, to make him stop worrying. He also asked Laurence to pray for Mr. Lewis, asking God to forgive him for worrying or harming any other children by his books and to help him not to do it anymore.[16]

Lewis observed that, in general, in his experience, children *do* catch on to Aslan's identity.[17] He certainly intended readers to make the transition from Aslan to Jesus. In another letter to a child, the eleven-year-old Hila, he tried to help her do so:

> As to Aslan's other name, well I want you to guess. Has there never been anyone in this world who (1) Arrived at the same time as Father Christmas. (2) Said he was the son of the Great Emperor. (3) Gave himself up for someone else's fault to be jeered at and killed by wicked people. (4) Came to life again. (5) Is sometimes spoken of as a Lamb (see the end of the *Dawn Treader*). Don't you really know his name in this world[?] Think it over and let me know your answer![18]

He was referring to a later volume in *The Chronicles of Narnia* titled *The Voyage of the Dawn Treader*, in which another group of children meet Aslan. One of them asks him if he is in their world too.

"I am," said Aslan, "but I have another name. You must learn to know me by that name. This is the very reason why you were brought to Narnia, that by knowing me here for a little, you may know me there better."[19]

CHAPTER 5

THE STONE TABLE

Atonement, Redemption, Justification

While Lucy, Susan, and Peter are enjoying their dinner with Mr. and Mrs. Beaver and hearing about Aslan, Edmund is simmering. He does not enjoy the meal. His craving for Turkish Delight has destroyed his appetite for ordinary, wholesome food. (Just as sinful pleasures can ruin the satisfaction we derive from lawful pleasures. Thus, pornography, adultery, or perversions can make marriage seem too mundane. Drugs can so stimulate the nervous system that the enjoyments of everyday life are rendered "boring.")

Edmund is treasuring up resentments against his brother and sisters, feeling that no one is giving him enough attention. The talk of Aslan is making him uncomfortable. So he slips out the door. The witch has given him directions to her house so that he can turn in the other three Children of Adam and Eve. Edmund slogs through the snow, rationalizing: "She won't really hurt them so much," he tries to make himself believe. "You can't believe what her enemies say about her.

Half of it is probably not even true. She is the rightful queen, after all. At any rate, she will be a better ruler than this Aslan."

"She treated me better than they do," Edmund thinks. As he trudges through the cold night, without a coat, which he left at the home of the beavers, he takes his mind off his misery by fantasizing about what he will do once the White Witch makes him king. He will make decent roads. He will install a private movie theater in his palace. He will get back at Peter by putting him in his place. Every time he slips and falls down, he thinks of his hatred of Peter, as if all his misery were Peter's fault.

> Some people are so in thrall to the Devil that they think God is so powerless he can be mocked.

Then, sure enough, Edmund arrives at the queen's house. In the courtyard, in the darkness, he makes out mysterious shapes that turn out to be statues covered with snow—creatures the witch has turned to stone. Among the stone creatures is a lion. Edmund thinks it is Aslan. He jeers at it—so much for mighty Aslan—and defaces the stone figure with graffiti, drawing a mustache and spectacles on it, a childish little act of vandalism that shows how some people are so in thrall to the Devil that they think God is so powerless he can be mocked.

Edmund then runs into a ferocious beast that he first thinks is a harmless statue but which turns out to be flesh and blood. It is a wolf, the head of the queen's secret police who had arrested Tumnus (now one of the statues). The wolf, snarling, takes Edmund to the queen. She does not treat him as kindly as she did before. She berates him for not bringing the others. Trying to get in good with her, Edmund tells her where they are and relates everything he heard at the beavers' house, including the news about the arrival of Aslan. Startled, the queen calls for her dwarf to prepare her sleigh at once.

Edmund begs for some Turkish Delight, but instead she gives him dry bread. Edmund is learning that sinful pleasures soon cease to be pleasures. All enjoyment ultimately comes from God, and only pleasures pursued in his will can give long-term satisfaction. What the Devil has in store for his servants is not pleasure (however much he may use superficial pleasure as a bait) but eternal suffering. In contrast, at God's "right hand are pleasures forevermore" (Ps. 16:11). Edmund is also learning what all sinners eventually learn: The Devil never keeps his bargains.

Sending a pack of wolves to the house of the beavers to kill anyone they find there, the White Witch takes Edmund onto her sleigh. Her dwarf drives the reindeer through the snow, headed for the Stone Table. Edmund's misery knows no bounds. He even misses Peter. He is appalled at the witch's cruelty and sees that she is not really on the right side after all. They come across a family of squirrels and other creatures celebrating Christmas. The infuriated witch turns them to stone. For the first time, Lewis notes in his narrative, Edmund feels sorry for someone other than himself.

> Edmund is waking up to his sinful condition.

Edmund is waking up to his sinful condition. The sleigh

gets bogged down in the slush of the melting snow. The dwarf recognizes that this is no thaw; it is spring, and it is Aslan's doing. The witch makes them all get out and walk. Edmund is bound. When he falters, he is whipped: "Everyone who commits sin is a slave to sin" (John 8:34).

"All Shall Be Done"

In the meantime, Lucy, Susan, and Peter have arrived at the Stone Table, where they meet Aslan, along with four centaurs, a unicorn, a pelican, an eagle, a large dog, and other denizens of Narnia who have become his retainers. Awed and overjoyed, the children are warmly received by Aslan, who welcomes them in a voice that banishes all their fears. (Just as God's Word consoles his people, the sheep who hear the voice of their Shepherd [John 10:3–5]. Notice how the Scripture describes the people as animals.)

> In the presence of Aslan, all tell the truth about themselves and take responsibility for the things they have done.

By this time the children have realized that Edmund has gone over to the witch. Peter confesses that Edmund's defection may have been partly his fault, that his anger may have contributed to making his brother go wrong. (This sequence begins the pattern that runs throughout *The Chronicles of Narnia*: In the presence of Aslan, all tell the truth about themselves and take responsibility for the things they have done—just as in the presence of God, there are no evasions.)

Lucy asks Aslan if anything can be done to save Edmund. "All shall be done," he replies, with a baffling look of sadness (p. 124).

Then Aslan takes Peter to a hilltop from which he can see the castle of Cair Paravel. Aslan tells him that within the castle are four thrones on which the children are destined to sit as the kings and queens of Narnia, and that he, as the oldest, will be the High King.

Suddenly, they hear a horn blowing, Susan's horn, meaning the company they have left behind at the Stone Table is under attack from the witch's wolves. Aslan sends Peter, with his sword, to earn his knighthood. (Notice that Aslan, like God, does not necessarily take his people out of the world's battles by some great act of power; rather, he equips them for battle and then sends them into the fray.) In the fight, Peter slays the wolf who heads the secret police. This is Peter's first battle. After it is over, Aslan knights him; and now the child gives way to the man.

Meanwhile, the White Witch, knowing that her spell over Narnia is subsiding, realizes how she can thwart the prophecy that four descendants of Adam and Eve will sit on the four thrones at Cair Paravel. If there are only three of them, the prophecy will not be fulfilled. All she has to do is kill Edmund.

She complains to her dwarf that the proper place to sacrifice Edmund is at the Stone Table, but she has Edmund—already in her power through his own sins—bound. The witch begins to sharpen her knife. She tells the dwarf to prepare the sacrificial victim. The dwarf opens Edmund's shirt collar and pulls back his head, baring his throat to her blade.

From this point on, Lewis begins to relate these events from Edmund's point of view. Suddenly we are in his mind, so it is as if all of this is happening to us, the readers. At the point when the knife is about to slit Edmund's throat, confusion breaks out, and Edmund finds himself taken up in someone's arms. A troop of unicorns, centaurs, and other Narnia creatures—sent by Aslan—rescues him.

Edmund is brought back, repentant. Aslan takes him aside for a long "conversation." Afterward—compare the convicting and restoring power of God's Word—Aslan gives the other children their brother back. He says that there is no need anymore to bring up the past.

Edmund apologizes to Lucy, Peter, and Susan. They all say that it is "all right." They are reconciled with each other. That should settle it. Hooray, hooray. Now everyone can "live happily ever after."

But it does not settle it. There is a debt that has to be paid.

The Witch's Claim

Before long, the White Witch sends her dwarf to seek an audience for her with Aslan. When she herself approaches, she announces to Aslan that he has a traitor in his midst. And, according to the Deep Magic from the Dawn of Time, every traitor belongs to her. And every treachery entitles her to a kill.

As a result, she maintains, Edmund belongs to her. His life is forfeit. She is entitled to his blood.

Mr. Beaver, a talking bull, and Susan all scorn what she says. But the witch points out that this law is carved onto the Table of Stone. It is written in letters as deep as the length of a spear on the World Ash Tree (which is, borrowing from Norse mythology, the foundation of the world). It is inscribed on the scepter of the Emperor-Beyond-the-Sea (that is, God the Father).

The Deep Magic is a divine, irrevocable law: "The wages of sin is death" (Rom. 6:23). Sinners in Narnia belong to the witch, just as sinners in our world belong to the Devil (1 John 3:8).

> The Deep Magic is a divine, irrevocable law: "The wages of sin is death" (Rom. 6:23).

"Surely you can do something to get around this law," suggests Susan, at which the great Lion turns fierce. He would never work against the will of his father the Emperor. Aslan agrees that what the witch says is true and that her claims on Edmund are valid.

And they are. And the Devil, whom she symbolizes, has equal claims on all of us. What is inscribed on the Stone Table is what is inscribed on the Tables of Stone brought down by Moses from Mt. Sinai: the Law. And because we have all violated that Law, we all belong to Satan, and we have all earned death.

The texts supporting this truth can be multiplied: "Cursed be everyone who does not abide by all things written in the Book of the Law, and do them" (Gal. 3:10). "Whoever makes a practice of sinning is of the devil" (1 John 3:8). "The law brings wrath" (Rom. 4:15). "Death spread to all men because all sinned [that is, broke the Law]" (Rom. 5:12).

Up to this point in *The Lion, the Witch and the Wardrobe,*

Edmund has been a minor villain. He is the bad boy—the bully, the sneak, the obnoxious brat—the sort most of us have had experience with or been. In Narnia, his faults are amplified as he becomes hooked on magical candy, falls in league with the witch, gets Tumnus turned into stone, and sells out his brother and sisters. But on the realistic plane, he remains just a boy with all-too-common faults.

Now, though, we relate to him on a different level. We are forced to identify with him. Lewis, in writing the story, tells portions of it from Edmund's point of view from the moment he first slipped out of the beavers' house until the confrontation between Aslan and the witch. That means that we readers have been put into his mind, seeing through his eyes. We, too, have done things similar to what Edmund has been doing—without the amplification of the fantasy framework—and we are glad that he has been rescued from the witch, straightened out by Aslan, and reconciled to his brother and sisters.

> The story here turns particularly powerful because now we can all relate to Edmund and his predicament.

But now we are reminded that Edmund does, in fact, belong to the White Witch, by his own free choice and as the result of his deliberate action. Despite his dramatic, last-second rescue from slaughter at the hands of the evil witch, he still remains under the death penalty for what he has done.

"But he is only a boy! What he did was not really that

bad," we may think. "Now he is sorry for what he did. Peter, Lucy, and Susan have made up with him. Can't we let bygones be bygones and pretend it never really happened?"

And this fantasy framework exaggerates everything anyway. In real life, in which we don't have to worry about being responsible for turning fauns into stone, Edmund's transgressions seem minor. "Granted, he is a rotten little boy," we reason, "but surely he will grow out of it."

The story here turns particularly powerful because now we can all relate to Edmund and his predicament. We have recognized his spite, his envy, his lusts for pleasure and revenge, his injured pride, because we, too, if we are honest, have succumbed to such sins ourselves. "You are slaves of the one whom you obey" (Rom. 6:16). Edmund is in that bondage of sin that leads to death. He stands condemned. The wages of sin must be collected.

The Passion of Aslan

As Aslan deliberates with the witch, Lucy is crying at the thought of what may happen to Edmund and all the talking animals are in a state of troubled silence. Then Aslan, after having sent everyone back so that he could talk to the witch alone, returns. To everyone's surprised relief, he reports that the witch has renounced her claim on Edmund.

The witch has an expression of "fierce joy" on her face. She asks how she can know Aslan will keep his promise. Whereupon Aslan roars—"Wow!"—so ferociously that she runs for her life. Aslan, like Christ, always keeps his Word.

An uneasy mood falls over the camp, as Aslan, himself distracted and sad, instructs Peter on what he must do as general in the battle to come. Peter has been assuming that Aslan will be there, but no, Aslan tells him, he cannot make that promise. Peter is shocked at the thought that Aslan will be absent, and he is frightened by the great responsibility being placed on his shoulders.

That night, Lucy and Susan cannot sleep. They are troubled at the strange sadness of Aslan. They get up in the night, where they see by moonlight Aslan walking away. They follow him.

His head bowed low and his tail dragging, Aslan is heading in the direction of the Stone Table. The girls run up to him. He says that he feels lonely and that he would be glad of company. They comfort him by doing what they had longed to do but did not have the nerve to do without his permission, burying their hands in his mane and stroking him like a cat.

Jesus too, on the night of his arrest, yearned for company: "My soul is very sorrowful, even to death," he told Peter, James, and John in Gethsemane. "Remain here, and watch with me" (Matt. 26:38). But while Lucy and Susan cannot sleep, the disciples of Jesus could not stay awake (vv. 39–45).

Then Aslan tells the girls he must go on alone. Hiding and watching, Lucy and Susan see Aslan go up to the Stone Table, where he is met by the witch and everyone on her side: Ogres, wraiths, demons, and creatures that, says Lewis, he won't describe because if he did, "grown-ups would probably not let you read this book" (p. 148). They hesitate at first, but then the witch laughs and commands that Aslan be bound.

The girls expect the lion to tear his tormentors to pieces, but instead he offers no resistance. Hags and evil dwarves and apes swarm over him, rolling him on his back and tying his legs. Similarly, in Gethsemane, "the band of soldiers and their captain and the officers of the Jews arrested Jesus and bound him" (John 18:12).

Then the witch has another idea. "Shave him!" An ogre with a pair of scissors runs up and starts cutting off his mane. Then they all make fun of him—"You're just a big old kitty cat"—and kick him, hit him, and spit on him. The girls sob as they witness this terrible humiliation.

Indeed, cutting off his mane is the way to humiliate a lion, and the scene parallels the stripping and mockery of Christ. But the shearing of Aslan underscores the fact that he is giving himself as a sacrificial victim and that the Lion is also a Lamb (Rev. 5:5–9).

> He was oppressed, and he was afflicted,
>   yet he opened not his mouth;
> like a lamb that is led to the slaughter,
>   and like a sheep that before its shearers is silent,
>   so he opened not his mouth. (Isa. 53:7)

The witch's minions drag Aslan onto the Stone Table, which we now recognize as being a sacrificial altar. The witch sharpens her knife, as she did when she was about to sacrifice Edmund. She raises her blade, but before she strikes, she exults over Aslan and rubs her victory in his face. "I will kill you," she tells

Not only does Aslan die for Edmund, he dies in Edmund's place. He takes the punishment Edmund deserved, just as Jesus did for us.

him, "but this will not save the human. With you dead, no one can protect him, and no one will be able to stop me from ruling all of Narnia forever. You have given your life for nothing. Despair. Die."

The girls hide their eyes at the moment of killing.

The whole scene parallels the moment when Edmund likewise was bound and his throat bared to the witch's blade. Not only does Aslan die for Edmund, he dies in Edmund's place. He takes the punishment Edmund deserved, just as Jesus did for us.

Easter in Narnia

Jesus was deserted by most of his followers after his arrest, during his crucifixion, and afterward, with the important exception of some of the women who followed him and remained faithful through it all: "Standing by the cross of Jesus were his mother and his mother's sister, Mary the wife of Clopas, and Mary Magdalene" (John 19:25). In a parallel fashion, these two little girls, Lucy and Susan, attend Aslan through his passion, death, and what comes next.

Victorious at the death of Aslan, the witch and her minions rush out to attack the now-unprotected Narnians. Lucy and Susan cry until, as Lewis puts it, there are "no more tears left." They tend to Aslan's body, taking off the muzzle and trying to wipe away the blood. The allusions are to the great subjects of Western art, the "deposition" (the taking down of Christ's body from the cross) and the *pietà*, a word meaning mercy that refers to a depiction of Mary cradling her Son's dead body.

Lewis gives his own distinctly Narnian touches to this artistic tradition. As the whole creation mourns, little mice swarm over Aslan's body to nibble off the ropes that held him, an act of service that will become important in a later volume, *The Voyage of the Dawn Treader*, which explains the bloodline of Reepicheep, the talking mouse.

The girls watch over the body through the night, walking back and forth from the Stone Table and the edge of the hill to keep warm. As the night changes to morning, the eastern sky turns red, heralding the rising of the sun. When the first golden light of the sun breaks through, the girls, their faces turned toward Cair Paravel, hear a loud noise.

Turning back, they see that the Stone Table has cracked and broken into two pieces. Aslan's body is gone. The girls start crying again, thinking someone has taken his body. Then behind them, they hear Aslan's voice. They turn around to see him alive.

Again, Lewis is closely paralleling the biblical accounts of the resurrection of Jesus. The women come to anoint the body of Jesus in the early morning (Luke 24:1). An earthquake unseals the tomb, and an angel rolls away the stone (Matt. 28:2). Finding Christ's body missing, the women first assume that someone has taken it (John 20:2). Mary Magdalene is crying, but she hears the voice of Jesus from behind her. She turns and sees Jesus (John 20:11–16).

One issue with the resurrection accounts is whether or not Jesus rose from the dead *bodily*, in the flesh. Gnostic heretics said that it was only the spirit of Jesus that rose. To this day, liberal theologians often deny the physical resurrection of Jesus, saying that the disciples simply experienced him "in their heart." But no. Christianity hinges on the physical death of Jesus followed by his physical coming back to life (1 Cor. 15:12–28).

The Gospels emphasize that the resurrected Jesus is no mere spirit, nor a ghost. He eats (Acts 1:4) and has his disciples touch him (John 20:24–28).

> As they were talking about these things, Jesus himself stood among them, and said to them, "Peace to you!" But they were startled and frightened and thought they saw a spirit. And he said to them, "Why are you troubled, and why do doubts arise in your hearts? See my hands and my feet, that it is I myself. Touch me, and see. For a spirit does not have flesh and bones as you see that I have." And when he had said this, he showed them his hands and his feet. And while they still disbelieved for joy and were marveling, he said to them, "Have you anything here to eat?" They gave him a piece of broiled fish, and he took it and ate before them. (Luke 24:36–43)

In Narnia, the girls also ask whether the Aslan they are seeing is a ghost. He responds, being a lion, in a catlike way. He licks their faces.

> If a willing victim innocent of treachery died in the traitor's place, the Stone "Table would crack and Death itself would start working backwards."

Jesus has risen in his physical body, but it is a resurrection body (1 Cor. 15:35–49). While he retains his wounds, his body has been changed, with new powers to pass through locked doors and appear and disappear as he wills (John 20:26–28). Similarly, Aslan has his mane back, is larger, is shining.[1] Yet the girls exult, "Oh, you're real, you're real!" (p. 159).

But what about the Deep Magic from the Dawn of Time? Aslan says that there is a deeper magic the witch knew nothing about, a Deep Magic from *Before* the Dawn of Time. It is true that traitors must forfeit their lives to the witch. But if a willing victim innocent of treachery died in the traitor's place, the Stone "Table would crack and Death itself would start working backwards."

The Deep Magic from Before the Dawn of Time alludes to one of the most mysterious, yet comforting texts in Scripture:

> Blessed be the God and Father of our Lord Jesus Christ, who has blessed us in Christ with every spiritual blessing in the heavenly places, even as he chose us in him *before the foundation of the world.* (Eph. 1:3–4)

God's plan of salvation—including the salvation of every believer—was established *before* he created the universe. Even before Adam and Eve fell, God in his omniscience had already planned the way he would be incarnate in that world to atone for their sins—and ours.

> In him we have redemption through his blood, the forgiveness of our trespasses, according to the riches of his grace, which he lavished upon us, in all wisdom and insight making known to us the mystery of his will, according to his purpose, which he set forth in Christ as a plan for the fullness of time, to unite all things in him, things in heaven and things on earth. (Eph. 1:7–10)

It is not necessary—or perhaps even possible, this side of

heaven—to comprehend fully what this passage means and what it implies. But the fact that God planned our redemption in Christ before our creation, to be carried out in the "fullness of time," means that even more fundamental than the Law that condemns us is the gospel that saves us. God is just, yes, but his grace and love are even deeper truths about his nature. Christ's saving purpose predates the Creation; the provision for the Atonement predates the fall; God's love for us predates our existence. The Deep Magic from the Dawn of Time is the Law; but the Deeper Magic from Before the Dawn of Time is the gospel.[2]

> The Law is no longer about how we are going to be punished for breaking it.

In Narnia, this Deeper Magic from Before the Dawn of Time, in which the Innocent becomes a willing substitute for the guilty, means that the Stone Table will be broken. That is, the Table of the Law—those hard, unyielding words inscribed in the stone tablets of Moses—will crack. Not that the laws inscribed on them will be cancelled; they are just fulfilled. Furthermore, as Peter Schakel points out, the "proper use" of the Law is now different: "Previously the Witch could claim the 'proper use' of the Stone Table was the execution of traitors; a broken table cannot be effective for, or symbolic of, that old use."[3] The Law is no longer about how we are going to be punished for breaking it. Edmund will no longer be condemned by the law inscribed on the Stone Table as deep as the length of a spear on the World Ash Tree. Nor, in real life, will those who have faith in Christ be condemned by God's moral law, despite the way they have violated it.

> But now the righteousness of God has been manifested apart from the law, although the Law and the Prophets bear witness to it—the righteousness of God through faith in Jesus Christ for all who believe. For there is no distinction: for all have sinned and fall short of the glory of God, and are justified by his grace as a gift, through the redemption that is in Christ Jesus, whom God put forward as a propitiation by his blood, to be received by faith. (Rom. 3:21–25)

This is the doctrine of justification by faith, which, in turn, rests on Christ's work of atonement (in which he suffered the punishment that we deserve), his redemption (in which he purchased us with his blood), and his resurrection (in which we are given new life).

There is no longer a need for sacrifice on our part. Christ has been sacrificed once and for all (Heb. 10:12–14). In Narnian terms, the Stone Table, a place of sacrifice, can be broken, since sacrifices are now finished once and for all.

The phrase "Death works backwards" refers to the great reversals that the message of Easter brings. Christ's death brings our

Now, our own death will become our entrance into everlasting life.

life: "For if we have been united with him in a death like his, we shall certainly be united with him in a resurrection like his" (Rom. 6:5). And now, our own death will become our entrance into everlasting life.

"The structure of the story," says Peter Schakel, "captures, for the imagination, the shape of the Christian message and presents it as true in Narnia as well: law first, then release, through sacrifice and love; first Deep Magic, then Deeper Magic."[4] And what Evan Gibson says about the action of the story can also be said of its theological meaning: "In *The Lion, the Witch and the Wardrobe*, we could almost say that Aslan does it all."[5]

After Aslan rises from the dead, Lucy and Susan join him in a joyous "romp"—running and leaping and chasing each other, as the children play with this great cat, who dandles them in his paws and tosses them safely in the air—expressing the intimacy and delight we can now have with the risen Christ.

But then the romp is finished, for a time. Aslan says he needs to get to business. He feels like roaring. He opens his mouth and gives a terrible roar that bends the trees. He has another work to accomplish.

Chapter 6

THE BATTLE

Sanctification and the Holy Spirit

Justification by faith is not the end of the Christian life. It is the beginning. And it is the continual energizing force for what comes next. God does not take us out of the world after he has saved us. He sends us back into the world. He does not take away all of our problems, trials, and conflicts. Rather, he turns them into occasions of spiritual growth. This is the doctrine of sanctification.

In this process, we live out our life, with its ups and downs, triumphs and failures. Through it all, we grow in holiness. This happens as the fruit of our justification through the ministry of the Holy Spirit.

The Lion, the Witch and the Wardrobe dramatizes how Christ won our salvation by dying in our place. It goes on to dramatize the work of the Holy Spirit and the dynamics of the Christian life.

The Breath of Aslan

In the two biblical languages of Hebrew and Greek, the word for "spirit" is essentially the same word for "breath" and "wind."[1] Thus, the Bible often speaks of the Holy Spirit in terms of these tangible images. These are theologically precise in, for example, presenting the Holy Spirit as the Breath of God. God's breath gives life. This is established at the very creation of man:

> Then the LORD God formed the man of dust from the ground and breathed into his nostrils the breath of life, and the man became a living creature. (Gen. 2:7)

The inspiration of the Scriptures by the Holy Spirit is described in terms of God's breath:

> All Scripture is breathed out by God and profitable for teaching, for reproof, for correction, and for training in righteousness, that the man of God may be competent, equipped for every good work. (2 Tim. 3:16–17)

And the gift of the Holy Spirit is given to Christ's disciples in one of his dramatic appearances after his resurrection when Jesus breathes on them:

> On the evening of that day, the first day of the week, the doors being locked where the disciples were for fear of the Jews, Jesus came and stood among them and said to them, "Peace be with you." When he had said this, he showed them his hands and his side. Then the disciples were glad when they saw the Lord. Jesus said to them again, "Peace be with you. As the Father has sent me, even so I am sending you." And when he had said

> this, he breathed on them and said to them, "Receive the Holy Spirit. If you forgive the sins of anyone, they are forgiven; if you withhold forgiveness from anyone, it is withheld." (John 20:19–23)

A related image associated with the Holy Spirit is wind. In Ezekiel's vision, the dry bones come to life when the wind gives them breath, and the Lord says, "I will put my Spirit within you, and you shall live" (Ezek. 37:14). And when the Holy Spirit was poured out on all the believers at Pentecost, "there came from heaven a sound like a mighty rushing wind" (Acts 2:2).

In Narnia, it is Aslan's breath, as he licks the girls' faces, that convinces them that he is "real," as in the role of the Holy Spirit in bringing people to belief (1 Cor. 2:10–14). Aslan's roar becomes a great wind that bends the trees, as if the Holy Spirit were let loose.

The children ride Aslan, who speeds to the witch's lair. Flying over the castle wall into the courtyard, they find themselves surrounded by what appear to be stone statues. They see the lion that Edmund had mistaken for Aslan. There are centaurs, unicorns, birds, foxes, dogs, satyrs, dwarves, and a towering giant. These, of course, are the witch's victims, whom she has turned to stone.

Aslan breathes on each of them, whereupon they transform from being stone to being flesh again. Lewis describes this transformation vividly, with the stone lion changing from white marble into his old golden color, like a piece of newspaper that gradually ignites into fire. As Aslan breathes on each statue in turn, the courtyard—once a place of dead quiet—erupts into a joyous cacophony of barking, neighing, roaring, and laughing, as all the talking animals, brought back to life by the breath of Aslan, gambol around him.

The curse of the witch is undone. This transformation from stone to flesh is a very biblical description of what happens when the Holy Spirit creates the new life of faith:

> And I will give them one heart, and a new spirit I will put within them. I will remove the heart of stone from their flesh and give them a heart of flesh, that they may walk in my statutes and keep my rules and obey them. And they shall be my people, and I will be their God. (Ezek. 11:19–20)

Lewis uses this same analogy of a statue coming to life in *Mere Christianity*, his classic defense of the truth of Christianity. He describes the difference between physical life and spiritual life. Adopting two Greek words, he says that *bios* (that is, physical life) is a matter of mere biology, while *zoe* (that is, spiritual life) comes from God.

> A man who changed from having Bios to Zoe would have gone through as big a change as a statue which changed from being a carved stone to being a real man.
>
> And that is precisely what Christianity is about. This world is a great sculptor's shop. We are the statues and there is a rumour going round the shop that some of us are some day going to come to life.[2]

Fighting the Battles

Finally, Lucy finds Mr. Tumnus, who had been turned into a statue by the witch and turned back into a faun by Aslan. Everyone is throwing open the windows of the witch's castle and letting in the light (1 Peter 2:9). The revivified giant takes his club and bashes open the gates; then he knocks down the towers and starts beating down the walls. The descriptions are of liberation—of freedom from the bondage of sin (John 8:34–36).

But this freedom has a purpose and a mission. The witch is still at large. She still must be defeated. Aslan organizes his newly alive followers into an army.

All this time, Peter, Edmund, and the talking animals on Aslan's side have been locked in battle with the witch and her forces. With the witch's supposed victory over Aslan, she has attacked his people in force. Peter and Edmund have been children up to this point, but now they are fighting as men.

The witch and her entourage of monsters are on the verge of overwhelming them. Those on Aslan's side seem very few. They are outnumbered. Statues litter the battlefield, creatures the witch has turned to stone with her wand.

When Lucy and Susan arrive, on Aslan's back, they see their brother Peter locked in hand-to-hand combat with the witch, he with his sword and she with her sacrificial knife. Edmund has been grievously wounded, though this once-rotten little kid, this former traitor who had sold out to the witch, has now performed heroically against her, breaking her wand with his blade.

Even after Aslan's death and resurrection, there is a battle to be fought. Even after Christ's death and resurrection, even after he has saved us, we Christians must continue to battle sin—in ourselves and in the world—and we must contend with the Devil.

The Bible uses the imagery of warfare to describe sanctification, as we see in the words of the apostle Paul: "I delight in the law of God, in my inner being, but I see in my members another law waging war against the law of my mind and making me captive to the law of sin that dwells in my members" (Rom. 7:22–23). But God gives us resources to fight these battles and to wage this spiritual warfare:

> Be strong in the Lord and in the strength of his might. Put on the whole armor of God, that you may be able to stand against the schemes of the devil. For we do not wrestle against flesh and blood, but against the rulers, against the authorities, against the cosmic powers over this present darkness, against the spiritual forces of evil in the heavenly places. Therefore take up the whole armor of God, that you may be able to withstand in the evil day, and having done all, to stand firm. (Eph. 6:10–13)

Paul goes on to employ allegory of his own, as he urges Christians to put on the belt of truth, the breastplate of righteousness, the shield of faith, the helmet of salvation, and "the sword of the Spirit, which is the word of God" (Eph. 6:14–17).

In these terms, Edmund has broken the witch's power to "harden people's hearts"—the very power that had paralyzed him—with that sword of God's Word, which conveys the Holy Spirit. Peter is battling the witch and her claims, represented by her sacrificial stone knife, with the same weapon.

The word for a story depicting this warfare is the Greek word *psychomachia*, meaning the battle of the soul. This was the title of a work by Prudentius, an early Christian writing in the fourth century, depicting a symbolic war between the Christian virtues and their opposing vices. Other literary authors and devotional writers have continued writing about *psychomachia*, from the allegories of Bunyan to the realistic internal struggles chronicled by Dostoyevsky. The tradition of the *psychomachia* lies behind the popular stories of warfare between "the good guys" and "the bad guys" and the common theme of "the battle between good and evil."[3] Lewis continues in this tradition; but with the battle coming right after the saving work of Aslan, he gives it the clear theological context of sanctification.

Though the battle is hard and the outcome seems uncertain, the victory has already been won. Aslan and his once-stone followers are racing to the rescue. Like the great cat that he is, he pounces on the White Witch.

Her fate is like that of Satan. At the fall, when the human race gave itself to Satan, God promised that the seed of the woman would someday bruise his head (Gen. 3:14–15). And Christ's victory over Satan will be repeated in the lives of everyone he has delivered from Satan's power: "The God of peace will soon crush Satan under your feet" (Rom. 16:20).

Back through the Wardrobe

The witch had looked back at Aslan with surprise and terror, but now she is dead. Most of her minions are killed too in the charge of Aslan and his companions, though some flee while others surrender.

Peter credits Edmund for saving their lives by breaking the witch's wand. Edmund is wounded, though, and at the point of death, but Lucy heals him with her Christmas present, the vial of healing elixir. Though Lucy gives him a few drops in his mouth, the device recalls the ancient Christian practice of anointing with oil, which was done for the sick (James 5:14) and sometimes as an accompaniment to baptism. This was considered symbolic of the anointing of the Holy Spirit.[4]

Once Edmund is healed, Lucy applies the elixir to the other wounded, as Aslan breathes on those whom the witch has turned to stone. Both actions allude to the Holy Spirit's role in repairing and restoring those who have been torn by sin and the Devil.

Now when Lucy sees Edmund, he looks better than she has seen him for years—since before he went to that "horrid school" where he first started to go wrong (p. 177). (Lewis himself saw from firsthand experience the corrupting influence of some of England's elite boarding schools, and he writes about the bad effects of certain modern educational theories every chance he gets in *The Chronicles of Narnia*.[5]) Now Edmund can look Lucy in the face. Aslan makes him a knight.

And then, Aslan takes the four children to the castle of Cair Paravel. He crowns them, and they take their places on the four thrones. Peter, Edmund, Lucy, and Susan rule as kings and queens of Narnia.

The Sons and Daughters of Adam and Eve take their rightful place as sovereigns over the world of animals. More than that, they symbolize the Christians' status as a "royal priesthood" (1 Peter 2:9), saints who "will judge the world"

(1 Cor. 6:2), who will receive "the crown of life" (James 1:12).

Aslan slips away, having, as Mr. Beaver explains, "other countries to attend to" (p. 180). He will often drop in, but he cannot be controlled. He is wild. He is not a tame lion.

> Aslan slips away. He will often drop in, but he cannot be controlled. He is wild. He is not a tame lion.

So King Peter, King Edmund, Queen Lucy, and Queen Susan reign for years and years. They still have battles to fight, problems to solve, and wise judgments to make. Evil things still lurk in the forest, and the bad giants still need to be conquered. But they fulfill their callings, ruling justly and well.

After having been kings and queens for so long, they start talking in "quite a different style," using "ye," "thee," "fair consorts," and other language from the medieval romances, whose world they now inhabit (pp. 182–184).

One day they go "a-hunting" for the White Stag, which they chase into a thicket. They see a great marvel, a tree of iron, as it were, topped with a lantern. This, as they say, "worketh" upon them strangely. Impelled by honor to seek the adventure, they go on, in the name of Aslan, farther into the thicket, where the branches give way to coats, and they come out through the wardrobe door into an empty room.

They are children again. They hear the tourists whom they all crowded into the wardrobe to get away from. They have come out at the same moment they left. Years have passed in Narnia, but no time at all has been taken up on earth. They have their whole lives to live out now in the ordinary world.

CHAPTER 7

COMING BACK HOME

The Spiritual Journey

The children entered the wardrobe and came out, transformed. In the wardrobe, they faced up to their personal responsibilities, encountered sin and grace, battled evil, and found a relationship with God. They (literally) grew. And yet, it all happened in an instant. Once out of the wardrobe, they were back to normal. Back to World War II. Back to the bad schools. Back to having to grow up.

From the outside—say, from the perspective of the tourists the children were hiding from if they had walked into the room—nothing external has happened. The children went into the wardrobe and then came out. In the tourists' eyes, nothing has changed. And yet, from the children's point of view, they have undergone something miraculous.

Real-life spiritual experiences are like that. No one can see another person's inner life. On the surface, little may be happening. A woman is sitting in a chair reading a Bible. A teenager is sitting in church, listening to a sermon. Ordinary life goes on. Science can find nothing special in the water of baptism or the bread and wine of Communion, nor may objective observers detect anything externally different in a person who has passed from unbelief to faith. And yet, in the person's hidden, spiritual life, something tremendous may have taken place.

Michael Ward makes the case that the whole device of the children's journey through the wardrobe is a symbol of spiritual awakening.[1]

We readers too, in picking up *The Lion, the Witch and the Wardrobe* and entering that book's world through our imagination, may have had a similar journey.

Edmund's Conversion

In another article, Michael Ward points to the odd fact that while *The Lion, the Witch and the Wardrobe* is all about how Aslan dies for Edmund, Lewis draws back from showing Edmund's response.[2]

In fact, there is a scene in which Lucy and Susan talk about whether or not to tell Edmund about what they witnessed Aslan do on his behalf. Susan thinks it would be "too awful" for him if he knew that Aslan died for him (p. 177). Lucy says that she thinks he still needs to be told.

But, of course, Aslan has already addressed Edmund personally, taking him aside before the witch made her claim and then presenting him back to the others, saying there is now no need to discuss the past, signifying that it has all been taken care of. While no one else ever learned exactly what was said, it was a conversation that Edmund would never forget. Thus, Edmund was converted through, as it were, the Word of

God. He was saved by the sacrifice to come, just as were the saints of the Old Testament.[3]

But why did Lewis not describe Edmund's response? Ward proposes several reasons. Maybe Lewis already thought he had enough redemption imagery, of which, as we have seen, the story is packed. More to the point, the true subject of the story is the work of Aslan:

> By dying for Edmund, Aslan did die for all of Narnia.

> Although technically speaking Edmund's betrayal and rescue are the two main events of the plot, yet it is the means of rescue that is thematically of the greatest importance. Aslan's death and resurrection are, within the world of Narnia, the central story, to which all other stories must defer and from which all other stories gain their significance. Furthermore, although Aslan apparently dies only for Edmund, it is conceded in later books that he died for the whole of Narnia, for if Edmund had been lost, the prophecy about the four thrones could not have been fulfilled and the White Witch would have ruled forever. It is therefore the story of Aslan that must dominate.[4]

By dying for Edmund, Aslan did die for all of Narnia. By dramatizing how Aslan is willing to die for a single person, Lewis shows how the death of Christ applies to the individual—to the individual reading the book.

Some people think of Christ's sacrifice as a vague abstraction that applies to humanity in general, but not to them individually, in their own individual sin and need.

But theologians have emphasized that if there had been only one person in existence, Christ would have died for that individual. And evangelists have emphasized that this is how each of us should think of Christ's sacrifice: that he died for us, personally.

Ward says that the other reason Lewis did not fill in the details of Edmund's response is that he wanted to create a blank slate "on which his readers could write their own story."[5]

Coming Back Home

Shakespeare wrote fantasies—the so-called romantic comedies. They follow a consistent structure: The characters are introduced in a real world that has become disordered, where parents and children turn against each other, where love has gone wrong, where the innocent are condemned to death, and where society is coming apart. Then the characters leave this disordered world for an enchanted forest or a mystical island across the sea. There, strange and magical things happen. Then the characters come back into the original world, transformed by what has happened to them in the magical world, and set it right again.

A Midsummer Night's Dream begins with a father demanding the death penalty for his own daughter for refusing to marry the man he has chosen for her. There, in Athens, everyone seems to be in love with the wrong person, and no one is loved back. When the couples flee into the woods, the fairies Puck and Oberon work strange transformations—from mixing up love potions to giving Bottom the Weaver a donkey's head—but at the end, everyone is back in Athens. The correct couples are together. Everyone's love is reciprocated. The father and the daughter forgive each other. Order is restored to the community.

The Tempest is about a duke named Prospero who is overthrown by his own brother and set adrift on a boat with his daughter to die. But the boat drifts onto an enchanted island, where Prospero cultivates wondrous powers. One day his evil brother comes sailing by. Prospero conjures up a terrible storm, a tempest, which causes the ship to wreck on this desert island. To make a long story short, bizarre things happen on that island. But the play ends with Prospero leaving his island and going home. His brother has repented and has been forgiven. His daughter is married to her true love. Prospero renounces his magic and returns to the ordinary world, whose order has been restored.

> We too come back from Narnia after we put down the book into our real, mundane, ordinary world. The glimpses we have had of redemption and sanctification and glory can be brought back from Narnia, into our own reality.

This is the kind of fantasy Lewis writes. At the end of every Narnia story (except for one), the children return to their world. But they have been changed, and they bring that change back into their realities. Edmund, as we will see in the later books, is not the same as he was when he first went into the wardrobe, even when he goes back to his "horrid school."

And, as readers, we too come back from Narnia after we put down the book into our real, mundane, ordinary world. The glimpses we have had of redemption and sanctification and glory can be brought back from Narnia, into our own reality.

What Next?

The story does not quite end with the children coming out of the wardrobe. Their consciences are still worrying them about those coats that were hanging in the wardrobe, which they put on as they went farther into the snow. They had rationalized that this act was not stealing, since they were not even taking them out of the wardrobe. But after all those years in Narnia, wearing armor and all, they lost track of the coats and did not bring them back. Now they feel that they must tell the Professor why the coats are missing. This decision, in turn, means that they must tell him everything.

And, surprisingly, he believes them. He tells them not to bother trying to get back into Narnia through the wardrobe to recover the coats; the coats are probably not any good after all those years in Narnia anyway. Besides, he says, they won't get back into Narnia through the wardrobe again.

So that means they *will* get back to Narnia again? "Of course," he says. "Once a King in Narnia, always a King in Narnia" (p. 186). But they will not get there by the same route as before. The Professor also tells them not to tell anyone else unless they are sure that they have been in Narnia too. They can know them, he explains, by odd things they will say and by a certain look they will have. (The Professor is one of this company, as will be seen in *The Magician's Nephew.*) And indeed, other children will be going into Narnia by different routes, as the other books of *The Chronicles of Narnia* unfold. As the book concludes, this may be the end of the adventures of the wardrobe, but it is only the beginning of the adventures of Narnia.

But the Professor also tells the children not to *try* to get back into Narnia. It will happen, he tells them, when they are not looking for it. That is to say, it is not a matter of works, but of grace. After all, Aslan is not a tame lion.

PART II:
THE FANTASY WARS

CHAPTER 8

CHRISTIANITY AND FANTASY

The genre of fantasy has become increasingly popular, both in children's literature and in books, TV shows, video games, and movies for adults. *The Lion, the Witch and the Wardrobe* is a classic in the genre, along with the entire *Chronicles of Narnia* series. But what about other fantasies? Many Christians embrace fantasies like *The Lion, the Witch and the Wardrobe* and *The Lord of the Rings*, but they object to others, like the extraordinarily popular *Harry Potter* books. What is the difference?

Some Christians object to *all* fantasy. They worry that any story featuring magic and the supernatural may be an opening to the occult. They believe that realistic stories are much better for both children and adults. Some go so far as to oppose fiction altogether. Fiction, they argue, means something that is untrue. Christians should only be interested in what is true. Thus they should read only biographies, histories, and other types of nonfiction.

Other Christians embrace *all* fantasy. Pastor Stan Bohall operates Quest Ministries, using the works of C. S. Lewis in seminars, courses, and other forums as a means of promoting evangelism and Christian growth. He points out that much Christian teaching is purely cognitive, consisting largely of abstractions and argumentation. But imagination is also an important means of grasping truth, a fact Christians often neglect, even though the Bible employs stories, imagery, and other appeals to the imagination.

> Imagination is also an important means of grasping truth, a fact Christians often neglect.

Bohall draws on theories about how the brain works (left brain = cognitive; right brain = imagination) and the notion that different people have different learning styles. He points out that C. S. Lewis makes the case for Christianity in terms of both modes of knowledge and learning styles, employing both argumentation (*Mere Christianity*) and imagination (*The Chronicles of Narnia*).[1]

He makes some good points and provides helpful resources for studying Lewis and using his works for Christian ministry. Although Quest Ministries concentrates on the works of Lewis, Bohall makes use of other fantasies as well. In a course description for a seminar titled "Fantasy Literature as a Tool for Evangelism," he explains:

> *The Chronicles of Narnia* convey an explicit Christian message. At Quest Ministries we believe that all fantasy literature conveys an implicit Christian message.

Mythologist Joseph Campbell concluded that all stories are part of the one story: once humans lived in Paradise; we were banished from Paradise; we are seeking to re-enter Paradise. C. S. Lewis and J. R. R. Tolkien wrote fantasy literature as an expression of this desire to enter the world we long for. You will discover how you can use interest in the *Star Wars* series, the *Harry Potter* series, *The Lord of the Rings,* and *The Matrix* as a way of conveying Christian truth to your friends.[2]

All fantasy, he maintains, stirs up the longing for heaven that is part of the human makeup. Even the stories of myth—though the basis for pagan religions and, as in Joseph Campbell, the neo-paganism cultivated by the New Age Movement—bring up repeated patterns (fall, trial, restoration; death, burial, resurrection) that point, even despite themselves, to Christian truth.

I agree that Christianity should not simply be reduced to a system of abstract ideas. After all, Christianity is not some bloodless philosophy; rather, it is unique among the world religions in how tangible it is: God became *flesh*; he died by torture on a cross; the Bible is paper and ink, expressing historical facts; Jesus has us employ water, bread, and wine to manifest his reality and his redemptive acts. As is already evident, I do believe the imagination can play an important role

> Christianity is not some bloodless philosophy; rather, it is unique among the world religions in how tangible it is: God became flesh.

in helping us come to terms with spiritual reality and in reaching people with the gospel. There really are universal themes in nearly all literature that are testimonies to our spiritual nature and that can be used to point to Christ.

And yet, I appreciate those who are worried about the use of fantasy. The allure of the occult and of those ancient pagan religions—which are reemerging in force in contemporary culture—does indeed pose dangerous temptations.

In the next two chapters, I will offer some comparisons between *The Lion, the Witch and the Wardrobe* and two other wildly popular fantasy series that are likewise crossing over into the popular culture via movies: *Harry Potter,* with its familiar controversy, and *His Dark Materials,* a work written in direct opposition to *The Chronicles of Narnia,* which evangelizes for atheism the way the Narnia books evangelize for Christianity. What follows (from here to the end of this chapter) is an article that I wrote in an attempt to sort out "good fantasy" from "bad fantasy." It surveys the distinctly Christian tradition of fantasy literature. It also suggests where to be careful.

This article first appeared as "Good Fantasy and Bad Fantasy" in *The Christian Research Journal,* volume 23, number 1 (2000), pages 14 to 22, and is reprinted with permission. It has been slightly edited.

Good Fantasy and Bad Fantasy

The *Harry Potter* books may be the biggest success story in children's literature. The series by a British woman named J. K. Rowling, who started writing them as a divorced single mother on welfare, has sold more than twelve million copies [by now, with more titles in fifty languages, that number is closer to 120 million], dominating the best-seller lists for more than two [now four] years. At one point, *Harry Potter* books ranked numbers one, two, and three, the first time one author had ever taken the top three spots. The fourth *Harry Potter* book was a best-seller based on advance orders alone—before it was ever published—and when it finally arrived, the whole publishing industry could hardly meet the demand.

Amazingly, most of these book buyers, who have taken over the adult best-seller charts, are children. Many of them, reportedly, are enjoying a book for the first time in their lives. Parents and teachers are saying that the *Harry Potter* series is turning on thousands and thousands of young people to the pleasures of reading. Boys, in particular, who have usually been more resistant to books than girls, are turning off the TV and the video games to spend time with a "good" book. Young people, said to have been conditioned by the TV attention span, are settling down with a seven-hundred-page book.

Surely, this is good news. Yet, something about the *Harry Potter* series makes Christian parents squirm: The novels are about a school for witches. Harry is a nerdy, miserable preadolescent raised by stepparents who despise him—until he goes off to Hogwarts School, a magical boarding school, where he learns to cast spells, becomes a star athlete in a broom-riding game, and enjoys fabulous adventures.

In a time when real witchcraft is in vogue, with Wicca chapters being recognized on university campuses as another legitimate campus ministry, these entertaining novels make witchcraft sound appealing. True, these broom-riding witches and wizards are a "good" version of fairy-tale characters—not the neopagan goddesses and nature worshippers of Wicca.

Nevertheless, Christian parents still worry that it could be a small leap from fascination with *Harry Potter* to overt involvement with the occult.

Harry Potter is only one example of how today's young people are awash in fantasy. Video games may be high-tech, but they often portray archaic realms of swords and sorcery. From Pokémon card games, they graduate to Magic the Gathering, then to other role-playing games, ranging from Dungeons and Dragons to Vampires. On TV they watch *Xena: Warrior Princess, Buffy the Vampire Slayer,* and *Sabrina the Teenage Witch.* Movies popular with children and teenagers are often science fiction–tinged fantasies, such as the *Star Wars* series, or contemporary redactions of old fantasy motifs, from genies in the bottle to talking animals.

> The challenge is to discern the difference between good fantasy and bad fantasy, recognizing not only its content but also its effects on the reader.

In fact, fantasy has always been a staple of children's entertainment, including the most wholesome. Fairy tales also have witches in them but are currently under attack by feminists and others for conveying values that are "too traditional." Some of the best Christian writers, from John Bunyan to C. S. Lewis, have used and defended the genre of fantasy. Lewis's *Chronicles of Narnia* have helped thousands of children and their parents understand the gospel.

The problem is not with fantasy, which is simply an exercise of the imagination. A work of fantasy can shape the imagination of its audience in either harmful or helpful ways. The challenge is to discern the difference between good fantasy and bad fantasy, recognizing not only its content but also its effects on the reader.

Harry Potter finally met his match in England when another fantasy character took over at the top of the best-seller list. A new translation of the tenth-century Saxon epic, *Beowulf*, rendered in vivid new prose by the Nobel Prize–winning Irish poet Seamus Heaney, also became a literary sensation. Both the new *Beowulf* and *Harry Potter and the Prisoner of Azkaban* contended for the prestigious British literary award, the Whitbread Prize. The nine-member panel that awarded the prize argued bitterly about which one was more deserving. A pro-*Beowulf* critic called the *Potter* book "derivative, traditional and not particularly well-written." A pro-*Potter* voter dismissed *Beowulf* as "a boring book about dragons."[3]

Both *Beowulf* and the *Potter* books are about dragons, monsters, and superhuman powers; yet the former is an acknowledged literary classic, while the latter is a controversial children's book. What is the difference? The Whitbread Prize, by the way, went to *Beowulf* in a five-four vote. What makes one kind of fantasy superior to another? How can a reader, or the parent of a reader, tell the difference between good fantasy and bad fantasy? Being able to make such judgments involves attention to the worldviews that lie behind the fantasies, an understanding of how fantasy works, and discernment of the effects a particular work of fantasy has on the reader.[4]

Fantasy and Reality

The answer is not simply to dismiss fantasy altogether in favor of works that are "realistic." One could argue that the current wave of realistic children's books is more negative in its effects than the *Harry Potter* fantasies. Books such as *Heather Has Two Mommies* by Leslea Newman and Diana Souza and *Daddy's Roommate* by Michael Willhoite are "realistic" attempts to legitimize homosexuality for four- to eight-year-olds. Other works in the genre of realism deal with divorce, child abuse, and sex. Popular titles written for teenagers include sympathetic treatments of drug abuse, running away from home, suicide, and premarital sex of every description.[5] Today's "realistic" world is one of bad parents, moral rebellion, and adolescent self-pity. The vogue for "realism" in children's books is often a pretext for politically correct indoctrination, antifamily diatribes, and angst-ridden problem narratives.

> The term "realism" begs the question of what one assumes to be real.

As a literary style, "realism" arose in the late nineteenth and early twentieth centuries as a manifestation of the worldview known as "naturalism." Authors such as Emile Zola, Frank Norris, and Stephen Crane insisted that writers should concentrate on what is "real"—that is, what can be experienced tangibly and empirically, the material universe explained by Charles Darwin and the social materialism set forth by Karl Marx. Their realism was bleak and depressing, filled with the seamy side of life, purposefully void of ideals, sentiments, morality, and, of course, religious values.

The term "realism" begs the question of what one assumes to be real. If one believes that Darwin's "law of the jungle" is real, then one will write stories about ruthless struggles for survival. A despairing view of reality leads to despairing works of art. Invariably, a particular author's "realism" is a function of his or her worldview. Moreover, since every work of fiction is, by definition, a made-up imaginary story, every work of fiction, no matter how realistic it seems, is a kind of fantasy.

The sunshiny view of homosexuality in *Heather Has Two Mommies* is written so that it seems real, but, in fact, it is a self-conscious projection of the author's imagination. Because it disregards the truths of God's commandments from a Christian perspective, it distorts rather than reflects reality. In leaving out the spiritual dimension, Zola's social commentaries may be realistic in their style, but they are not real at all.

A realism that confines itself to descriptions of only those things that can be seen in ordinary life necessarily excludes that which remains unseen but which nonetheless gives ordinary life its meaning—namely, truths of morality, faith, and transcendent ideals. The challenge for a Christian writer or artist is how to get at these invisible truths. It is possible to show their effects in a realistic way or to go inside the heart of the characters to show their inner struggles. There are realistic Christian authors, such as Dostoyevsky, but another

> By definition, fantasy is wholly imaginary. It is not reality, but it can provide a way to think about reality.

way to write about these invisible truths is to explore them symbolically; that is, through fantasy. By definition, fantasy is wholly imaginary. It is not reality, but it can provide a way to think about reality.

One of the first explicitly Christian discussions of literature was *An Apology for Poetry* written in the sixteenth century by the statesman, soldier, man of letters, and devout Protestant Sir Philip Sidney. He took on the Puritan Stephen Gosson's charge that poetry—by which he meant creative, imaginative fiction—is a lie, since it recounts things that are not real.

Sidney argued that imaginative fiction is one of the few expressions that cannot be a lie. "To lie," he observed, "is to affirm that to be true which is false." A fiction writer, however, never pretends that his tale actually happened. "He nothing affirms," said Sidney, "and therefore never lieth."[6]

Historians, philosophers, and scientists can hardly avoid lying sometimes—that is, stating something to be true that is really false—even if their lapse is inadvertent. But a fiction writer, by definition and as everyone knows, is working with what is imaginary. He or she is describing not what is or has been but what could be or should be, writing "not affirmatively but allegorically and figuratively."[7]

The work of fiction, says Sidney, is "profitable inventions." It is profitable precisely because it can deal with ideals, "what should be," and it is especially effective in teaching morality. A good story, Sidney says, both teaches and delights. In other words, it teaches by delighting.[8]

The Christian psychologist William Kirk Kilpatrick has shown how stories shape children's moral education. Children are taught the attractiveness of virtue and the repulsiveness of evil not so much by abstract precepts—and certainly not by schools' "values clarification exercises"—but by rooting for virtuous heroes and being inspired by a good story to emulate their behavior.[9]

> If stories can make virtue attractive to some, they can also make vice attractive to others.

Logically, it seems that the reverse would also be true. If stories can make virtue attractive to some, they can also make vice attractive to others. Like all powerful tools, literature can have a good use or a bad use. If one's purpose is to teach a child not to lie, nothing beats "The Boy Who Cried Wolf." Aesop's other fables, for all of their talking animals, convey true notions of hard work ("The Ant and the Grasshopper") and persistence ("The Tortoise and the Hare").

Many Christian writers from Dante to J. R. R. Tolkien have, in fact, favored "profitable inventions" over realistic or even nonfictional tales. One reason, lying deep in the biblical imagination, may have something to do with one of the Ten Commandments. The prohibition against making "graven images" specifically forbids the making of "likenesses": "Thou shalt not make unto thee any graven image, or any likeness of any thing that is in heaven above, or that is in the earth beneath, or that is in the water under the earth" (Exod. 20:4 KJV).

For the classical Greeks, who gave us our aesthetic heritage, the essence of art is *mimesis*, the imitation of external reality. For Plato, the visible world itself is nothing more than an imitation of ideal forms in the transensory realm of ideas. The Hebrews, on the other hand, saw the universe as a creation by a transcendent God. By extension, art is seen as a creation by a human being.

The commandment would seem to make realistic art, the aesthetic tradition of *mimesis* that makes imitations of the external world, problematic. Of course, the commandment is actually aimed at idolatry, "bowing down" to these likenesses as practiced by the pagan nature religions. The Bible, in fact, required that certain kinds of realistic art—renditions of lions, pomegranates, seraphim—be made to adorn the temple. But the Jews took the prohibition of likenesses to heart. This did not prevent them from making artistic designs, but it did prevent them from making realistic designs. The pottery and coins of early Israel are decorated with nonrepresentational designs—intricate intersecting lines and geometric shapes—which are beautiful, though they are likenesses of nothing in heaven or on earth or in the water.[10]

The early church attacked the idolatry of classical paganism by insisting that the pagan mythologies were not real but only stories; that is, fantasies. In fact, one could argue that the early Christians invented fantasy—or even invented fiction—by what they did to myth. They taught that the myths were not historically true, while retaining them in their educational curriculum as pure stories.

"It was the Christians," observes Werner Jaeger, "who finally taught men to appraise poetry by a purely aesthetic standard—a standard that enabled them to reject most of the moral and religious teachings of the classical poets as false and ungodly, while accepting the formal elements in their work as instructive and aesthetically delightful."[11]

The pagans did not believe the sagas of their gods were fictional myths. They believed they were literally true. But for Christians to believe that Icarus actually flew so high on wax wings that they were melted by the chariot of the sun god would be idolatry. Once it is clear that there is no sun god and that this story never really happened, it can be appreciated in a different way as an illustration of what can become of human pride.

Children who have a strong sense of fictionality and who know that there is a difference between the story and the actual world are inoculated against most of the bad effects of fantasy. It is when the child takes the fantasy world as the real world—that is, when it ceases to be fantasy—that problems can arise. When the child understands the difference between fiction and reality, however, stories of all kinds can both teach and delight.

Good Escape and Bad Escape

Another Christian defender of fantasy, who himself was one of the greatest fantasy writers of them all, was J. R. R. Tolkien. One charge against fantasy is that it is mere "escapism."

Tolkien, however, pointed out that it is not always morally irresponsible to try to escape. "Why should a man be scorned," he wrote, "if, finding himself in prison, he tries to get out and go home? Or if, when he cannot do so, he thinks and talks about other topics than jailers and prison walls?"[12]

There is a difference, he said, between "the flight of a deserter" and "the escape of a prisoner."[13] It is indeed possible to be a "deserter" by using fantasy to escape from one's true responsibilities and one's God-given place in life. This would be a misuse of fantasy. But Tolkien was emphasizing the sense in which today's materialistic worldview—which admits of no God, no immortality, no moral truths, no transcendent ideals—is, in fact, a narrow, stifling prison house.

In an intellectual and cultural climate that recognizes nothing beyond what can be seen, touched, and measured, it may take a fantasy—such as Tolkien's *Lord of the Rings*—to awaken people's imaginations to longing, beauty, moral heroism, and transcendent ideals. Working on their imagination in this way might waken a sense in them that there is something more to life than a narrow material universe of buzzing atoms.

Part of the problem with today's variety of unbelief is that people cannot imagine any kind of transcendence. C. S. Lewis, the great Christian apologist whom Tolkien was instrumental in bringing to Christ, cited as a key moment in his spiritual pilgrimage his reading in a railway station the odd adult fairy tale *Phantastes* by the nineteenth-century Christian author George MacDonald. "I did not yet know (and I was long in learning) the name of the new quality, the bright shadow, that rested on the travels of Anodos [the main character of the book]. I do now. It was Holiness.... That night my imagination was, in a certain sense, baptized; the rest of me, not unnaturally, took longer."[14]

Lewis went on to write fantasies himself such as *The Chronicles of Narnia*. One of the *Chronicles, The Voyage of the Dawn Treader,* features a boy named Eustace Scrubb, a product of permissive, liberal parents and the modern educational system. Being brought up a materialist, he liked only books that were realistic. "He liked books if they were books of information and had pictures of grain elevators or of fat foreign children doing exercises in model schools."[15]

When Eustace finds himself in Narnia, with its talking animals and noble ideals, he is utterly lost. Rude, obnoxious, and self-centered, Eustace cannot function in a moral world. Then, he confronts a dragon. Since "Eustace had read none of the right books," he does not even know what it is. "Most of us know what we should expect to find in a dragon's lair," writes Lewis, "but, as I said before, Eustace had read only the wrong books. They had a lot to say about exports and imports and governments and drains, but they were weak on dragons."[16] Partly due to this ignorance and to the twisted quality of his own moral nature, Eustace eventually turns into a dragon himself.

> Lewis's point is that reading "the right books" can equip a child to recognize the dragons that lurk outside and within.

Finally, the mighty lion, King Aslan, destroys Eustace's evil nature, and Eustace is reborn, a repentant sinner redeemed and changed by Lewis's symbol for Christ. Eustace needed to "escape" from his materialistic self-centered worldliness into the larger, freer, more spacious world—not just of Narnia but of spiritual reality, which, though it cannot be fully seen, can be evoked, experienced, and symbolized.

Lewis's point is that reading "the right books" can equip a child to recognize the dragons that lurk outside and within. *The Chronicles of Narnia* are some of those "right books" that can shape a child's spiritual awareness far better than realistic books about grain elevators.

G. K. Chesterton wrote about "the ethics of Elfland" and how fairy tales convey a way of thinking that accords well with the Christian worldview:

> There is the chivalrous lesson of "Jack the Giant Killer"; that giants should be killed because they are gigantic. It is a manly mutiny against pride as such.... There is the lesson of "Cinderella," which is the same as that of the Magnificat—*exaltavit humiles* [the humble will be exalted; Luke 1:46–56]. There is the great lesson of "Beauty and the Beast"; that a thing must be loved before it is lovable. There is the terrible allegory of the "Sleeping Beauty," which tells how the human creature was blessed with all birthday gifts, yet cursed with death; and how death also may perhaps be softened to a sleep.[17]

These lessons are not mere abstract precepts; rather, they are attitudes and insights that sink deep into the imagination and help shape one's character.

The child psychologist Bruno Bettelheim reports how he has found fairy tales useful in treating children scarred by trauma and abuse.[18] The "scary parts" of fairy tales, he maintains, anticipate children's actual fears (as in Hansel and Gretel's parents' being unable to provide for them—children do worry about things like that!). They then show how, despite trials (getting lost in the woods) and temptations (don't eat the candy house!), through courage and virtuous action (Gretel's outsmarting the witch), they can "live happily ever after."

While much contemporary children's literature tries to project a "safe" domestic world and insists that even fairy tales have their scary parts and harsh punishments sanitized out of them, Bettelheim takes a different view:

> Adults often think that the cruel punishment of an evil person in fairy tales upsets and scares children unnecessarily. Quite the opposite is true: such retribution reassures the child that the punishment fits the crime. The child often feels unjustly treated by adults and the world in general, and it seems that nothing is done about it. On the basis of such experiences alone, he wants those who cheat and degrade him ... most severely punished. If they are not, the child thinks that nobody is serious about protecting him; but the more severely those bad ones are dealt with, the more secure the child feels.[19]

The world of the fairy tale is a realm of rigorous moral order. When used rightly, fantasies can help instill that moral order into a child's personality.

Fantasizing Evil

Since fantasies can have a beneficial effect in stimulating the imagination in a constructive way, it must also be possible for other fantasies to stimulate the imagination in a destructive way. One tale might convey the attractiveness of moral heroism; another might be an occasion to wallow in evil thoughts.

It is not enough just to look at what the story is about. Some parents object to C. S. Lewis's *The Lion, the Witch and the Wardrobe* just because it has a witch in it. Never mind that the book presents the witch as a repellent villain, indeed as a symbol of the Devil and his temptations. Never mind that the book is a powerful allegory of the gospel. The mere presence of the witch is assumed to make the book and its readers partake of the occult. One might just as well say that a tract against witchcraft is occult since it mentions the word.

Nor is the answer simply to throw out all stories that contain violence. There can be no plot without some kind of conflict. There can be no story in which everyone just lives happily all the way through. There must be some kind of problem, some obstacle to overcome, some conflict, whether external (good guys versus bad guys) or internal (the character having to make a decision between two options) or both (the character having to decide which side to be on). Fantasies tend to externalize inner states or to symbolize ideas in concrete form. That means the conflict will usually be presented as external. This is manifested in fights with monsters, in battles, and in chivalrous contests. These can all be characterized as "violence." Yet without conflict, one can have accounts of only grain elevators. Imaginative wrestling with conflicts is exactly how stories teach morality and build character.

Today, it is nearly always the liberal humanists who deny the real difference and the conflict between right and wrong, who object the loudest to the "violence" in fairy tales.

Slaying a dragon violates animal rights; rescuing a princess is sexist. Eustace's parents, who protected him from books about dragons, were well-intentioned and informed by their philosophical bent as vegetarians and pacifists.

Fantasies, along with all literature, must be evaluated according to their meaning and their effect. What does the violence mean? Does it dramatize the conflict between good and evil, or does it glorify the strong terrorizing the weak?

What is the effect of the violence on the reader? Does it make the reader less likely to hurt people in real life? Or, does it stir up the pleasures of cruelty and sadism?

> What is the effect of the violence on the reader? Does it make the reader less likely to hurt people in real life? Or, does it stir up the pleasures of cruelty and sadism?

The point of view—that is, the view of the story's character through whom the narrative is filtered and with whom the reader is made to identify—is a useful point of analysis. Traditional stories nearly always present the point of view of the "good guy." (In more complex realistic stories with an internal conflict, the character may not be so simple, and the story may be precisely about a moral struggle. Tragedies show a noble character whose downfall comes from a moral flaw; but in fantasies, the characters are usually more simple.) Contemporary stories, on the other hand, often place the reader with the point of view of a character who is evil.

Bram Stoker's *Dracula*, the original vampire novel of the nineteenth century, was from the point of view of the virtuous characters who were battling the monster. Dracula was "the other," who was distant and repulsive. Yet modern vampire treatments, including Anne Rice's best-sellers and the various role-playing games, typically present the point of view of the vampires. Readers imagine what it is like to sink their teeth into someone and drink their blood. Both Bram Stoker and Anne Rice have written fantasies "about" vampires, but the imaginative experience and the moral effect they create are far different.

In today's video games, a popular format is the "first-person shooter." "First person" refers to the point of view. This type of interactive game presents the action through the eyes of a character within the story, who happens to be the player. The video screen depicts what the character is seeing. The player is a "shooter" because he or she is put into the role of a killer who strides through a virtual landscape, raising a gun, aiming it at cowering victims, and then blowing them away.

Some games are high-tech shooting arcades, pointing at nonhuman targets, whether alien spaceships or clearly unreal monsters. Those games are probably relatively harmless. Some first-person shooters, however, are imaginative re-creations of what it would be like to be a serial killer. (Incidentally, as has been well publicized, the Columbine killers liked these kinds of games, and later they reenacted the games in real life.)

It is argued that the number of players who actually act out their games in real life is miniscule. Christians, however, know that it is not just the actions but the thoughts and imaginations of the heart that are morally corrupting. Jesus himself emphasized that God judges murderous thoughts as well as murderous actions; that adultery committed "in [the] heart" violates God's commandment, even if it is never acted upon (Matt. 5:21–22, 27–28).

What we fantasize about—as occasioned by literary experience—is spiritually important. Pornographic imaginings and fantasizing about hurting others are indeed harmful, even if they are never acted out, because they corrupt the heart.

Another difference between traditional fantasies and some that are popular today is that the former have clear demarcations between good and evil, while the latter do not always make this distinction. Today, the boundary between good and evil is often blurred or erased. Bram Stoker lived in a moral, biblically informed universe—vampires were powerless against crosses and other Christian symbols. Today's vampire movies usually acknowledge no such authority, with Dracula simply swatting the crucifix away in one film. Anne Rice goes further, making us feel sympathy for the vampire, who emerges as more "noble" than his victims. Other fantasies—whether in books, films, or video games—set up a morally neutral universe in which no side is

> Just as a tale of chivalry can inspire ideals of courage and honor, the sword and sorcery sagas of raping and pillaging, with no moral center, can deaden the heart.

any better than another, with every man and every monster for himself. In still others, evil simply reigns supreme.

If fantasy can be used to teach moral truths and carry them into the imagination, it is also possible for fantasy to desensitize the moral imagination. Just as a tale of chivalry can inspire ideals of courage and honor, the sword and sorcery sagas of raping and pillaging, with no moral center, can deaden the heart.

For Christians, the main concern about certain kinds of fantasy is the danger of occultism. Though fantasy sets up its own self-contained worlds in which marvelous things can occur, preoccupation with magic, spirits, and sorcery can be spiritually deadly. The temptation can be to reverse literary history and turn fantasy back into myth and myth back into paganism.

If witches were merely fantasy creations, they would be harmless. But witchcraft is real. Demonism, necromancy, and pagan rituals are not fantasies; they are real. Someone may be fascinated with such things in fantasy literature and then go on to practice them in real life. We now have vampire fans who have graduated from Anne Rice novels to role-playing games to actual drinking of other people's blood.

Again, the problem is crossing away from fantasy, what the reader knows to be imaginary, into the actual world, what the reader believes to be real. The ability to tell the difference between fantasy and reality is an essential survival skill. In fact, it is a definition of sanity.

Since fantasy grows out of the inner world, its overall danger—when it is dangerous—has to do with the temptation to sink into oneself, to indulge one's sinful imagination (Gen. 8:21), and to wallow in the darkness of our fallen nature. The pseudorealism of a false worldview also shuts us into darkness. Good fantasy, on the other hand, takes us out of ourselves, countering our darkness with at least a glimpse of the external light.

The Case of Harry Potter

So what are Christians to think about the *Harry Potter* sensation? First of all, there is good reason why so many children are enamored with these books, and why they are making so many children excited about reading for the first time. This is a clear symptom of imagination deprivation. It is also a powerful indictment of our educational system.

To use Tolkien's metaphor, children's imaginations are imprisoned, and they are right to want an escape. Their schools often lock them into a politically correct curriculum, earnestly trying to inculcate in them a consciousness of "real" and depressing social problems. Their textbooks are materialistic, with science texts asserting the closed naturalistic system of evolution, with history texts attacking even the remnants of American ideals, and with reading texts spinning out "problem" stories and moral dilemmas. No wonder children hate to read.

The key to the popularity of the *Harry Potter* books is not that they are fantasies—there have been many of those that are not nearly so popular—but that they are books about school. Children read about Hogwarts School with a sense of recognition. Here are the cliques, the pressures, and above all the struggle for popularity with which they are all too familiar. But here the school is at least interesting. Instead of just making them sit around in groups and share their feelings, this school teaches them wonderful things (how to become invisible, how to change things with a magic wand, and how to fly)!

Children, especially bright children, can identify with Harry Potter, who at first is trapped in the "Muggle" world (the drab ordinary material realm of those who cannot see the supernatural), while alienated in his school and feeling despised even in his stepfamily. It turns out he is really a wizard all along, and at Hogwarts this nerdy kid with glasses even becomes popular! Young *Harry Potter* fans are not so much fantasizing about witches as they are fantasizing about being popular and successful.

The Christian case against *Harry Potter* is that Harry is in a school for witches. Christians know that witches are not just fantasy characters, but that they are real; whether as overt Satan worshippers or as the neopagan devotees of Wicca.

Defenders of *Harry Potter* can point out that the Hogwarts witches have nothing to do with the Wicca or black magic kinds of witches. They are not evil at all, nor do they preach any kind of New Age nature religion. These witches are out of the fairy tales, with brooms and spells, except that they are good (as in the "good witch" in *The Wizard of Oz*). Actually, Harry is learning to be a "wizard," such as Gandalf in Tolkien's *The Lord of the Rings*, not a warlock (the male version of a witch).

Still, at a time when witchcraft is becoming a major presence in our youth culture with books about how to be a witch targeted at teenagers, Christians are right to be concerned. In fairy tales, witches are typically "wicked," reinforcing the clear lines between evil and good: that is, the forces of darkness and the forces of light. Anything that blurs those lines is cause for concern.

Harry Potter, however, does not erase the lines completely. There is an overtly evil power in Voldemort: a true wicked witch with whom Harry and his schoolmates are in conflict throughout the series. Some see disrespect for parents in Harry's bad relationship with his Muggle aunt and uncle, who make him sleep in a closet; but, in fact, Harry's real parents were killed (by Voldemort), and his love and admiration for them is a major part of his character.

So, yes, *Harry Potter* arguably falls short in some regards, though it is not nearly so bad as some (such as the vampire craze or the first-person shooters or the how-to witch books). If the book spoke only of wizards—a profession found only in fantasy books—rather than the clear-and-present danger of witchcraft, most of the problems would evaporate. Christian parents are right to be cautious of their children's enthusiasm for the series. Yet, if the *Potter* bug has already bitten their children, they should handle the situation with care.

> Christianity is not a narrow, materialistic, boring worldview such as the one satirized in the *Potter* novels and taught in today's schools.

Parents need to make clear that Christians are not Muggles. In other words, Christianity is not a narrow, materialistic, boring worldview such as the one satirized in the *Potter* novels and taught in today's schools. It is Christianity that has the open universe with room both for the natural and the supernatural, for the ordinary and the miraculous. It is Christianity that recognizes unseen truths of goodness and beauty and that believes in a genuine battle between the forces of darkness and the forces of light. The account of how God became man in Jesus Christ, defeating Satan and atoning for our sinfulness by dying on the cross and rising again, is the most wonderful, mind-blowing story of all—having the profound advantage of also being true. The Bible asserts it, history confirms it, and the Holy Spirit brings us to believe it. Those who think in biblical terms have a far bigger, more stimulating worldview than any of their materialistic and occult competitors.

> A child who knows about dragons—and witches—from "the right books" will know to stay away from them and will know that he or she doesn't want to become one.

The best way to inoculate children against being confused by *Harry Potter* or seduced by the fantasies that are far worse, in addition to giving them a solid grounding in the Word of God, is to expose them to good literature, including good fantasy. To use C. S. Lewis's terms, a child who knows about dragons—and witches—from "the right books" will know to stay away from them and will know that he or she doesn't want to become one.

CHAPTER 9

THE LION AND THE MUGGLES

I f you are a *Harry Potter* fan, I am not going to argue with
you. My own rather nuanced position on the controversy—
which has led pro-*Potters* to think I am against the books and
anti-*Potters* to think I am for the books—is set forth in the pre-
ceding chapter.[1] But this book is about *The Lion, the Witch and
the Wardrobe*. Some facets of a work can best be seen by setting
it next to another work of its kind. Noticing the similarities
and differences can bring out what is unique about both
works and can reveal dimensions that may not be evident
when the work is considered by itself.

Comparing the *Harry Potter* books to *The Chronicles of
Narnia* shows a number of distinctive elements in both series
and in the approach to fantasy taken by C. S. Lewis and J. K.
Rowling. Some of them are obvious—for example, the overt
Christian content in Lewis's books—but others go to the heart
of what a particular fantasy can mean and what it can do.
What is most revealing about a comparison of the two series

> In the Narnia books, though, the stimulating, mind-blowing fantasy does not condescend to the realm of the ordinary and the normal, but rather ends up valuing it and shedding light on its meaning.

is the different attitudes that emerge in them toward ordinary life.

The *Harry Potter* books contrast the world of the "Muggles," those boring and clueless ordinary folks who know nothing of magic, to the wonderful world opened up by Hogwarts School, where witches and magic offer a splendid and thrilling alternative to the everyday routines of mundane, normal existence. In the Narnia books, though, the stimulating, mind-blowing fantasy does not condescend to the realm of the ordinary and the normal, but rather ends up valuing it and shedding light on its meaning. The fantasy works in the service of everyday life.

Two Witches

The most searching critiques of the *Harry Potter* books have been those written by Richard Abanes. It is significant to note that while Abanes is severely critical of the *Potter* books for glorifying the occult, among other things, he nevertheless says that fantasy as a whole is a very positive genre in the moral and intellectual development of children and adults.

He defends the writings of J. R. R. Tolkien from Christians who think *The Lord of the Rings* trilogy also glorifies the occult, and he shows how different Tolkien's fantasy is from that of Rowling.[2] Abanes also thinks highly of C. S. Lewis and *The Chronicles of Narnia*.[3] So I will leave the deeper theological analyses to Abanes and focus instead on some simpler points of comparison.

First, the two works do have significant similarities. Both have children as main characters. Both employ the device of parallel worlds, with a magical realm coexisting side by side with the ordinary realm. In both works characters go back and forth between the worlds, usually by means of an ordinary object that proves to be a threshold into the other world (whether a wardrobe or a mysterious track in a train station). Both works are highly stimulating to the imagination. Both works set up a conflict between good and evil.

In *The Lion, the Witch and the Wardrobe*, the witch is the villain. In the *Harry Potter* books, witches are heroes. Actually, there are different kinds of witches in Rowling's novels, with some being good and some "practicing the dark arts"; but being a witch, in itself, is neutral, a matter of some individuals having magical abilities that can be developed at educational institutions such as Hogwarts School of Witchcraft and Wizardry.

One can make the case that the witches in *Harry Potter* are not really the same as the Devil-worshipping kind of witches, or even the feminist neopagans of the Wicca movement. It may be said that Rowling is using the word "witch" in a new sense, even though she retains the black cats, broomsticks, and spell-casting of the folk culture. But even if this were true—and setting aside the issue of glamorizing witches at the very time that both the Devil-worshipping and the neopagan variety are coming back into the culture—it is clear that Lewis is following the fairy-tale tradition of the wicked witch in a way that Rowling is not.

Rowling is using elements of the fairy-tale tradition (black hats, flying brooms, spell-casting) to make up something new (a sorting hat to make residence hall assignments at the witch boarding school; quidditch matches). Frank Baum in *The Wizard of Oz* also employed "good witches." Rowling does not feel bound to the literary and folkloric conventions that require the "wicked witch."

> Lewis, though, is making perhaps an even more important point, that evil, in fact, is often attractive.

Lewis, though, does follow the fairy-tale conventions and the historical meaning of the word ("one that is credited with usu. malignant supernatural powers; *esp.*: a woman practicing usu. black witchcraft often with the aid of a devil or familiar"[4]). This usage tells us that Lewis is more of a traditionalist than Rowling, that he is culturally more conservative.

Not that he is just repeating the old conventions. Most witches in the old stories are ugly. Lewis's White Witch is beautiful. What the traditional stories are trying to get at in depicting witches or other villains as being ugly is that evil should be seen as repulsive. Lewis, though, is making perhaps an even more important point, that evil, in fact, is often attractive. Since Lewis's tale is about temptation, a fall, and the conflict between appearance and reality, making his witch beautiful advances his themes. (When fairy tales also take up such themes, they can be similarly flexible. The witch in "Snow White," a story that likewise explores how appearances can be deceiving, is also a beautiful queen.) Usually in folklore, black symbolizes evil and white symbolizes goodness, so that witches wear black hats and black cloaks and have black cats. But *The Lion, the Witch and the Wardrobe*, reinforcing the point that we must not judge by appearances, is about a witch garbed all in white.

Two Schools

A less obvious point of comparison suggests that Lewis, while being more conservative than Rowling, is actually being more subversive, as far as children are concerned. Rowling is pro-school. Lewis is anti-school.

That is to say, the *Harry Potter* books glorify the elite British boarding school, where the aristocracy, the wealthy, and the upwardly mobile middle-class families send their children when they turn ten, an institution that Lewis hated. Rowling's fantasy is all about how wonderful it is to leave your boring family, where no one understands you, to go live instead at a marvelous school, where you get to spend all of your time with people your own age, form friendships, and achieve popularity by playing sports.

In Lewis's books, though, having to go off to a boarding school means having to leave your family where you are loved, living with strangers who do not understand you, getting bullied, and being constantly humiliated for being bad at sports. Young Lewis was shipped off to boarding school when he was ten, about the same age as Harry Potter. In his autobiography, *Surprised by Joy*, Lewis describes how miserable he was at boarding school. He was homesick, bullied, and, because he was no good at sports, treated like an outcast. He did love learning, to be sure. He writes with warmth and appreciation of the tutors who, in effect, homeschooled him at school. But, he writes, "The putting on of the school clothes was, I well knew, the putting on of a prison uniform."[5] Boarding school he describes as a "prison." And getting to go home for the holidays, to him, was like paradise.

> Life at a vile boarding school is in this way a good preparation for the Christian life, for it teaches one to live by hope. Even, in a sense, by faith; for at the beginning of each term, home and the holidays are so far off that it is as hard to realize them as to realize heaven.[6]

When children read Lewis, they feel understood.

"And yet, term after term, the unbelievable happened," he wrote, as the time counted down "and the almost supernatural bliss of the Last Day [of school] punctually appeared."[7]

Lewis had a remarkable capacity to remember his childhood and what it was like to be a child, an ability that made him a great children's author. When children read Lewis, they feel understood.

When he was older, he attended a more notable boarding school, where he had to face the social hierarchy that teenagers tend to establish. Here is what Lewis had to say about the "Bloods" at his school, that is, the popular set:

> The most important qualification is athletic prowess.... [and] good looks and personality will help. So, of course, will fashion.... A wise candidate for Bloodery will wear the right clothes, use the right slang, admire the right things, laugh at the right jokes ... those on the fringes of the privileged class can, and do, try to worm their way into it by all the usual arts of pleasing.[8]

Lewis went on to tell about the cruelty of this social hierarchy—all the bullying, hazing, beating, and other kinds of domination—citing, too, the role played by homosexuality in this all-boys' school.[9]

Harry Potter, of course, thrives in this atmosphere. His quidditch wins alone make him one of the most popular boys in the school, let alone the reputation he always carries with him as someone particularly gifted and that lightning scar that marks him as being fated for greatness. For Harry, his home life is miserable, with his parents dead and his having to be raised by an aunt and uncle who hate him. Of course, for Harry and those like him, school can be a glorious escape. And the fact that Harry is so good on the flying broom and achieves such popularity and has such a "brilliant" career at school is part of the fantasy, with great appeal, too, to young readers who are not that way, but who fantasize what it might be like.

By the same token, for children like young Lewis who are happy at home, having to leave their families for boarding school is indeed horrible. Children like Lewis, who are not good at cricket or rugby or whatever and who are not popular or fashionable, those who are at the bottom of the pecking order, of course, hate life at boarding school. Some children thrive in this kind of school while others do not. Some children may fantasize about being at such a school, and some may fantasize about escaping from it.

The point here is that the *Harry Potter* books exalt the boarding school culture—which is not necessarily all that different from the culture of the non-boarding schools that Americans are more used to—whereas C. S. Lewis, in both his nonfiction and his *Chronicles of Narnia* criticizes it. In *The Lion, the Witch and the Wardrobe*, part of the blame for Edmund's turning traitor is ascribed to "that horrid school which was where he had begun to go wrong" (p. 177), where he had learned bullying, cruelty, and viciousness. ("You've always liked being beastly to anyone smaller than yourself," Peter tells him, "we've seen that at school before now" [p. 42].) Once Edmund is converted, and the children become kings and queens of Narnia, one of their royal deeds, proving the beneficence of their reign, is that they "liberate ... young dwarfs and young satyrs from being sent to school" (p. 180).

In the later *Chronicles of Narnia*, the criticism of the boarding school culture continues. In *The Voyage of the Dawn Treader*, Eustace is so twisted by the materialistic thinking instilled into him by his "modern" school that he can hardly function in Narnia, which he hates with a passion. "Eustace Clarence liked animals, especially beetles, if they were dead and pinned on a card. He liked books if they were books of information and had pictures of grain elevators or of fat foreign children doing exercises in model schools."[10] Not having "read the right books," he turns into a dragon, until he too, like Edmund, is saved and changed by Aslan. In *The Silver Chair*, the children get into Narnia, not through a wardrobe, but by being chased by school bullies.

One reason that *Harry Potter* has struck such a chord with young people is that its culture—revolving around school, friends, sports, and popularity—is their own. Hogwarts School, of course, is much more interesting than their schools are, but they can easily identify with Harry and his social scene, which includes both his troubles at home and his adventures at school. Even if many of the millions of his readers are not happy in their own school's culture, here is a better one that they can enjoy vicariously.

The *Harry Potter* books are, in fact, examples of a once-popular genre of children's literature, the "school story." Books such as *Tom Brown's School Days* described life in a boarding school, with emphasis on a hero's exploits on the playing field and in the dormitories. Lewis wrote about them, contrasting school stories, unfavorably, to the fairy tale. "I never expected the real world to be like the fairy tales," he wrote. "I did expect school to be like the school stories."[11]

Lewis contrasts the kind of "escapism" and "wish-fulfillment" offered in school stories to the sort found in fairy tales:

> There is no doubt that both arouse, and imaginatively satisfy, wishes. We long to go through the looking-glass, to reach fairy land. We also long to be the immensely popular and successful schoolboy or schoolgirl.... But the two longings are very different. The second, especially when directed on something so close as school life, is ravenous and deadly serious. Its fulfillment on the level of imagination is in truth compensatory: we run to it from the disappointments and humiliations of the real world: it sends us back to the real world undivinely discontented. For it is all flattery to the ego. The pleasure consists in picturing oneself

the object of admiration. The other longing, that for fairy land, is very different.... It stirs and troubles him (to his life-long enrichment) with the dim sense of something beyond his reach and, far from dulling or emptying the actual world, gives it a new dimension of depth. He does not despise real woods because he has read of enchanted woods: the reading makes all real woods a little enchanted.[12]

> The boy reading the fairy tale is happy in the very desires it kindles, "for his mind has not been concentrated on himself, as it often is in the more realistic story."

Lewis says that "the boy reading the school story of the type I have in mind desires success and is unhappy (once the book is over) because he can't get it." The boy reading the fairy tale is happy in the very desires it kindles, "for his mind has not been concentrated on himself, as it often is in the more realistic story."

Lewis insists that he is not against school stories as such. He might well have appreciated how J. K. Rowling in the *Harry Potter* series worked fairy-tale elements into the genre of the school story. But he says that school stories are more like the escapist fantasies that psychologists worry about than are fairy tales.[13]

Lewis's books, though, while seemingly more traditional and conservative than Rowling's books, undercut those old school values, such as group solidarity, conformity, and pride of person, position, and place. Children, with their own school experiences to relate to, can enjoy them both, but Lewis is arguably more subversive. The *Harry Potter* books are about an escape to school, while the Narnia books are about an escape from school.

Two Real Worlds

The great divide in the *Harry Potter* books is between the witches and the Muggles, between those who are oriented to the exciting, mystical, other-worldly realm of magic and those who know only their dull, boring, mundane material existence, empty of wonder and joy. We have Hogwarts School with its enchantments and its supernatural surprises, and we have Harry's home, dominated by unimaginative adults trapped in a drab existence in an ugly, utilitarian house where Harry has to sleep under the stairs. Muggles cannot see the magic around them. Magic vehicles fly through the air and pass through walls, but Muggles are oblivious to such wonders, continuing to slog through their narrow little lives without noticing anything else.

The figure of the Muggle is actually a great symbolic creation. There are people like the Muggles. From a Christian perspective, these are the materialists who cannot accept the reality of anything beyond what they can see and test and measure, and so reject the supernatural truths of faith. From a literary perspective, these are people who could use a good dose of fantasy to jump-start their imagination and their sense of wonder.

The problem is that the *Harry Potter* books treat Muggles with a sense of condescension. It isn't a matter of even trying to win them over. The magic the young students are given consists largely of mean tricks to pay back the Muggles in their dismal lives. In the world of the *Harry Potter* books, the universe is divided into those who "get it" and those who don't.

The Gnostic heretics of old thought that way, that there are an elite few who enjoy secret knowledge and occult power, and the masses of the unenlightened who are not worth considering. The Gnostics also rejected the objective, external, material world—to the point of rejecting the doctrines of the creation and the incarnation—in favor of a misty, internal spirituality unconnected to the physical world. Thus, *Harry Potter*, like *The Da Vinci Code* and other culturally popular artifacts, has its Gnostic elements.

> Lewis always affirms ordinary existence as something good and wholesome and precious.

Lewis, by contrast, in both his nonfiction and his fiction, always affirms ordinary existence as something good and wholesome and precious. In his autobiography, he tells how his friend Arthur Greave taught him to appreciate, in literature and in life, the quality of "Homeliness." He started reading books by Jane Austen and other early nineteenth-century realistic novelists to supplement his reading in fantasy.

> The very qualities which had previously deterred me from such books Arthur taught me to see as their charm. What I would have called their "stodginess" or "ordinariness" he called "Homeliness"—a key word in

his imagination. He did not mean merely Domesticity, though that came into it. He meant the rooted quality which attaches them to all our simple experiences, to weather, food, the family, the neighborhood.... This love of the "Homely" was not confined to literature; he looked for it in out-of-door scenes as well and taught me to do the same.[14]

The Chronicles of Narnia, those noted fantasies, are filled with moments of "Homeliness," times of savoring ordinary life. Notice, for example, the scene with Mr. and Mrs. Beaver: the company trudging through the snow and seeing the smoke coming from the fireplace of the warm home that will welcome them; Mrs. Beaver working on her sewing machine; the simple but delicious meal of fresh fish, boiled potatoes, "creamy milk," and a mar-

> J. R. R. Tolkien says, if you are in a prison, it is healthy to want to escape.

malade roll. Compare that meal and the other homely meals celebrated by Lewis throughout his books with the spectacular, extraordinary feasts in the *Harry Potter* books, which are closer to having Turkish Delight at every meal.

Escape and Return

As J. R. R. Tolkien says, if you are in a prison, it is healthy to want to escape.[15] Your real-life world may be so constricting and stifling, so Muggle-like, that breaking out into a total fantasy world where anything can happen can be exhilarating.

But if you simply escape the prison in your mind, you are still in prison. Giving up on everyday reality, accepting the conventional existentialist wisdom that external reality is all meaningless, is a grim conclusion. Reading a fantasy and letting your imagination fly can give you a little mental break from Mugglehood. But nothing is changed.

Young Lewis, stuck in his awful schools and imprisoned even more in his materialistic worldview, had always loved fantasy literature. It gave him an escape. But when he picked up George MacDonald's *Phantastes* in that train station, he was introduced to fantasy with a different effect. Before, he said, he had always sought a bright light beyond this world. This time, reading this fantasy, it was as if a bright light were shining on *this* world.[16]

This fantasy did not merely allow him to escape the prison. It tore down the prison.

As has been said, Lewis's Narnia stories follow Shakespeare's fantasies by beginning in a rather bleak, realistic world (the Battle of Britain during World War II), leaving it for a different world of marvels but also trial, and then coming back home, the characters transformed. This is a major difference between *The Chronicles of Narnia* and the *Harry Potter* books. Though Harry comes back to his miserable life with his Muggle family between terms, his true home is with the witches. In Narnia, the characters (with one important exception at the very end of the series) come back to their families, and their true home can be found in ordinary life. The readers of *The Lion, the Witch and the Wardrobe* certainly come back into their own mundane world when they close the book. But afterward—at least in the experience of many readers—that world seems less Muggle-like.

CHAPTER 10

THE ANTI-LEWIS AND THE ANTI-NARNIA SERIES

There are four major fantasy series today that are beloved by children and adults alike. Three of them we have already talked about: *The Chronicles of Narnia* by C. S. Lewis; *The Lord of the Rings* by J. R. R. Tolkien; and *Harry Potter* by J. K. Rowling. The other one is *His Dark Materials* by Philip Pullman. All of them are by British authors. All have sold millions and have inspired passionate followings. All have been made into major motion pictures, increasing their presence in the culture.

The *Harry Potter* books have provoked controversy, particularly among Christians, for various problematic elements. Strangely, despite their great popularity, *His Dark Materials* has not provoked nearly the discussion or the alarm. J. K. Rowling has disavowed any negative themes that some have found in her books, and she insists that she too is a Christian. She sees herself, rightly or wrongly, following in the tradition of Tolkien and Lewis. But Philip Pullman is

> What Lewis was doing for Christianity—writing a fantasy to win over children and adults to his faith—Pullman is doing for the cause of atheism.

doing something completely different. What Lewis was doing for Christianity—writing a fantasy to win over children and adults to his faith—Pullman is doing for the cause of atheism.

This is not an accusation, nor is it reading things into his stories, as so often happens—rightly or wrongly—with the *Harry Potter* books. This is Pullman's express and admitted purpose.

In 2001, with the completion of his trilogy, Pullman won the Whitbread Prize, Britain's top book award, the first time the author of a children's book was ever so honored. "This year's Whitbread prize-winner Philip Pullman is, as you might expect, a fine writer and he's a fine writer with a cause," commented one writer. "His cause, as he himself has made clear, is to destroy Christianity and to liberate the world from any faith in the Christian God."[1]

Pullman has been described as "the new Lewis," in the sense that he is a master of children's fantasy as Lewis was and that what he is writing reflects "new" ideas.[2] More precisely, he is better understood as "the anti-Lewis."[3] As such, setting *His Dark Materials* next to *The Chronicles of Narnia*—to the extent that they are polar opposites—will illuminate both works. More than that, it will illustrate what fantasy is capable of and demonstrate the worldviews that are currently contending for the imagination of both adults and young people.

Hating Narnia

"I hate the Narnia books," says Philip Pullman, "and I hate them with deep and bitter passion."[4] *The Chronicles of Narnia*, he says, are "one of the most ugly and poisonous things I have ever read, with no shortage of nauseating drivel."[5]

He hates them not just because he dislikes their style or is annoyed by the notion of talking animals. He does not hate them for aesthetic reasons or because of his own personal taste, in the way that some people "hate" onions or soap operas. He hates them because he thinks they are evil. "The Narnia books lead up to a view of life so hideous and cruel I can scarcely contain myself when I think of it."[6] "I think [Lewis] was actually dangerous."[7]

Some Christians think *Harry Potter* is dangerous. But even the most stereotyped, fundamentalist, book-burning censor would probably not go so far as this liberal, supposedly tolerant former schoolteacher in his outrage against—and his fear of—*The Chronicles of Narnia*.

Why does he hate them so much? His specific complaints are odd and vague. He says the books are "racist and sexist." This is the charge that postmodernists are always making against conservatives, with little to back it up. Where is the racism? He must be thinking of the Calormene who appear in later books, parallel to the Saracen of medieval romance, the Muslim enemy of the chivalrous knights. This may be politically incorrect these days, despite the war on terrorism, but it cannot be racism. As Peter Hitchens observes, referring to a character in *The Last Battle*, "One of Lewis's noblest characters is the dark-skinned Calormene, Emeth, while the vilest is the White Witch."[8] As for sexism, Pullman must think that the books are too traditional when it comes to the role of women. But Hitchens quotes Michael Ward, who points out that the central character in *The Lion, the Witch and the Wardrobe* and in *The Chronicles of Narnia* as a whole is Lucy:

> Lucy Pevensie is unquestionably the most prominent and morally mature character in the narrator's eyes. Lucy is the first of the children to discover Narnia, and is described as more reliable and more truthful than her brother Edmund. She is the one who most often sees Aslan, the Christ-figure.[9]

> Lewis's stories "view childhood as a golden age from which sexuality and adulthood are a falling-away."

Pullman also complains that "these books celebrate death" because in one of the later books some children die, in a scene that emphasizes their everlasting life in heaven.[10] It is odd that he is so squeamish, given the violence and child-killing in his own novels. A more specific charge is the view of childhood in Lewis's stories, "with their view of childhood as a golden age from which sexuality and adulthood are a falling-away."[11] But this could be said of nearly every children's book.

It is evident, especially from reading *His Dark Materials*, that what Pullman most hates is the Christianity in *The Chronicles of Narnia*—that, coupled with Lewis's conservative sensibility, his appreciation for (as we discussed in the last chapter) what is ordinary, what is normal. Pullman, in his left-wing politics and his bohemian intellectualism, tends to look down upon what he would consider "middle-class values." In his books, Hitchens observes, "The bad are to be found among the religious, the respectable and the well-off."[12]

But it is Christianity that fills Pullman with the most antipathy. He believes it is oppressive, judgmental, and life-denying. But he did find one thing in Lewis's Narnia books to appreciate. He told an audience consisting mostly of children that when he first read Lewis's Narnia series, he realized that what Lewis was up to was writing propaganda in the cause of the religion he believed in.[13] Pullman considered it "propaganda in the service of a life-hating ideology."[14] But he apparently realized that what Lewis could do, he could do also. He decided that he could write propaganda in the cause of what *he* believed in.

His Dark Materials

The trilogy *His Dark Materials* consists of these novels: *The Golden Compass* (also titled *Northern Lights* in the British editions), published in 1996; *The Subtle Knife*, published in 1997; and *The Amber Spyglass*, published in 2000. All sides concede that Pullman is a skillful writer and a good storyteller. Some say he is a better storyteller than a propagandist, that they can enjoy his tales while dismissing his anti-Christian rants.[15]

Indeed, his stories have many of the elements of classic fantasy, and even of Narnia. There are talking animals. A bear plays a prominent role in the first book, though most of the animals are "daemons"—a moth, a dog, a lizard—which, in at least one of his worlds, are visible manifestations of a person's soul. (Pullman is not afraid to draw on traditions of the witch's "familiar" or of overt "demons.") As in *Harry Potter*, there is a school setting (Oxford University and the imaginary Jordan College). There are also lots of witches, all of whom are on the side of what is right, according to the story. As in Tolkien, there are wonderful made-up words (gobblers, gyptians, alethiometer, cliff-ghasts) and names (Lyra, Iorek, Cittagazze, gallivespians, Metatron).

There is even a wardrobe. Just as Lewis first got the idea for his stories from a mental image of a faun with packages, an image that kept running through his head, Pullman had the image of a girl hiding in a wardrobe.[16] And so, much as in Lewis's book, his story begins, with Lyra in a wardrobe. Only instead of going through the wardrobe into a new world, Lyra looks out from the wardrobe to witness the beginnings of a sinister plot.

What unfolds from there is a rousing tale with a complicated plot that defies retelling, featuring warring angels, zeppelins, ghosts, harpies, kidnapping, quests, and intrigue. Whereas Tolkien's fantasy world is completely self-contained, and whereas Lewis imagines a world parallel to our own, Pullman's universe consists of other worlds so numerous they cannot be counted. One goes to them by using "the subtle knife" (also named "God-killer") to carve windows into the air, which then give access to the other worlds. (If the fantasy concept of "other worlds" is analogous to the realm of the mind and the imagination, as we have argued, Pullman's device of an infinite number of worlds corresponds well to the postmodernist assumption that truth is relative. Since "we all have our own truths," everyone, in effect, inhabits a world of his or her own.)

But holding the story all together are connections to the plot of *Paradise Lost,* John Milton's great Christian epic on the war in heaven between Satan, with his rebel angels, and the hosts of Michael, loyal to the Son of God, and the temptation and fall of Adam and Eve. But Pullman, following some radical critics, as we will discuss later, is on the side of Satan, presenting the story of Satan's rebellion—and that of Adam and Eve—as a valiant struggle for liberation against oppression.

> Pullman is on the side of Satan, presenting the story of Satan's rebellion—and that of Adam and Eve— as a valiant struggle for liberation against oppression.

His Dark Materials—the title being a quotation from Milton's epic, as we will discuss— is about an eleven-year-old girl named Lyra, who lives in a parallel world to our own, who, in the first novel, embarks on a quest to rescue a friend who has been kidnapped and, more importantly, to learn the secret of a mysterious "dust." The second novel focuses on another character, a boy from our world named Will, who links up with Lyra and gains possession of "the subtle knife," with its ability to cut windows into other worlds. In the third novel, we learn that Will and Lyra are the new Adam and Eve.

Through it all are the machinations of Lord Asriel, whom Lyra thinks is her uncle, but who turns out to be her father and then is revealed to be something far more. "Lord Asriel is gathering an army," we are told in *The Subtle Knife,* "with the purpose of completing the war that was fought in heaven aeons ago."[17] "There is a war coming, boy. The greatest war there ever was. Something like it happened before, and this time the right side must win."[18] This is the war between Satan and the hosts of God. Lord Asriel is the Satan figure. He is the hero of *His Dark Materials*, and his is presented as "the right side."

Here is why Pullman thinks Satan was right to rebel against God and how he looks at the continuing conflict today:

> There are two great powers ... and they've been fighting since time began. Every advance in human life, every scrap of knowledge and wisdom and decency we have has been torn by one side from the teeth of the other. Every little increase in human freedom has been fought over ferociously between those who want us to know more and be wiser and stronger, and those who want us to obey and be humble and submit.[19]

God, in *His Dark Materials*, though often referred to as "God," is called the "Authority." He is cruel and tyrannical, always wanting to limit every kind of freedom, knowledge, and joy.

"The Christian religion is a very powerful and convincing mistake," says heroine Mary Malone, a lapsed nun, "that's all."[20] As for the church, this is the sect of all who are evil. In Lyra's world, there was never a Reformation, so the church is all Catholic, but with shots at the Protestantism in our world as well. The pope is named John Calvin. The Vatican has moved to Geneva. Thus, Pullman is able to bring together and to caricature the two church traditions he detests the most: Roman Catholicism and Calvinism. The resulting church he portrays with all of the stereotyped bigotry of the old anti-Catholic Know-Nothing Party: priests in black robes sneak around murdering people, launching sinister conspiracies, and staging inquisitions.

At the end—and I am leaving out a plot crammed with incidents, twists, and marvels—the Authority (that is, God) is defeated. Will and Lyra find him in a crystal litter. He turns out to be nothing more than a senile old man. He is so old and feeble that he doesn't know what he has been doing. They help him out, whereupon he is so frail that the light and the air make him break up into nothingness. That is to say, if the concept of God is exposed to the light of reason and the fresh breeze of progress, he disappears.

And then can emerge what Lord Asriel has been fighting for—and in fact gives his life for, since, Gandalf-like, he saves the children from the Authority's mighty angel Metatron by wrestling the two of them into an abyss: the Republic of Heaven. Not the "Kingdom of Heaven," which entails hierarchy, lordship, obedience, and the dreaded "Authority," but "the Republic of Heaven," in which everyone is equal and free. At the very end, Will and Lyra, the new Adam and Eve, realize that since there are so many worlds, so much diversity built into creation, that a literal Republic of Heaven is not possible. But the trilogy ends with this exhortation:

> "We have to be all those difficult things, like cheerful and kind and curious and patient, and we've got to study and think and work hard, all of us, in all our different worlds, and then we'll build ... the Republic of Heaven."[21]

The Republic of Heaven is within us.

Pullman's Contribution to Atheism

The great achievement of Philip Pullman, the significance of which should not be underestimated, is that he manages to make atheism appealing to the imagination.

A relatively small percentage of people in the world today are out-and-out atheists. A great number of people today have false religions, they make up their own feel-good theologies, or they complacently assume that "the God I believe in" will always be nice to them without their having to pay much attention to him. But they believe in *some* kind of deity.

> The great achievement of Philip Pullman, the significance of which should not be underestimated, is that he manages to make atheism appealing to the imagination.

The problem with atheism is that it is so bleak, so *depressing*. If there is no God, then there is no basis for right and wrong, no basis for meaning in life, and no hope for a better life after this one. The material world is all there is. When we die, we rot. That fact has a way of taking the luster off the short time we have on this earth. We are born, we grow up, we reproduce, and we die. That's it.

Honest atheists, such as Jean-Paul Sartre, face these grim implications forthrightly. There is no God, said Sartre, so we must face up to the fact that life has no meaning. In the face

of the absurdity of exis-
tence, he said, we must create our own meaning in the
little time we have left and
face with courage the ultimate nothingness.

It is no accident that most fantasy writers, with their sense of wonder and transcendence, have been religious.

Atheism may appeal to
the reason of many people,
but it lacks an imaginative
appeal. The main imagina-
tive attraction may be to
rebellion against the status
quo, a condescending sense of superiority to ordinary folks in
their bondage to religion, an ironic and cynical stance toward
life, all of which appeal to some people.

In twentieth-century literature, atheistic writers favored
stark realism, to the point of naturalism, stressing that the
material world is all there is, that every higher ideal is an illusion, and that we are only animals, caught up in our deter-
ministic destiny created by our instincts of sex and violence
and by the cruel practicalities of survival of the fittest. Other
atheistic artists have cultivated "absurdism," unveiling the
meaninglessness of life by playing with grim humor with the
meaninglessness of their own art.

It is no accident that most fantasy writers, with their sense
of wonder and transcendence, have been religious. Fantasy as
a genre is usually ridiculed by atheists as "escapism," an idealistic illusion weak people dream up as a way to avoid facing
the absurdity of this hard, cold reality in which we are stuck.

But what Philip Pullman has done in writing an atheistic
fantasy is to make atheism imaginatively stimulating. He

makes atheism sound inspiring, hopeful, liberating, moral, and even spiritual.

Central to his books are those dark materials, the "dark matter" or "dust" that the characters are trying to track down and to understand. This "dust" turns out to be the stuff of love and consciousness. In fact, it turns out that everything is made out of this dust, which is the essence of both spiritual and physical existence. There is no creation in Pullman's universes. The Authority had claimed to have created everything out of nothing, but, in reality, everything is made of dust. The dust, not God, is the uncreated source of existence. The old, decrepit deity is nothing but the oldest angel who precipitated out of dust, as has everything else.

This is nothing more than classic materialism, of course, which insists that matter is all there is, so that everything that exists is made out of particular tiny bits of matter called atoms. Even the first recorded atheist, Democritus, who disbelieved in the Greek gods, believed that the material world consisted of atoms, coming up with the theory far before the development of nuclear physics. According to this materialistic worldview, the universe is made of atoms. That is to say, dust.

Furthermore, atheists maintain that matter—and, hence, nature—is eternal. "You Christians say that God is eternal, having always existed, without a creator," they say. "Why can't nature have those same qualities?" In the golden age of scientific materialism, the late 1800s, atheists argued that the natural order as we perceive it today just always existed. Twentieth-century astronomy, which uncovered evidence that the universe did have a beginning, the "big bang," shook that belief. But in the version accepted today, before the big bang, all the matter in the universe existed in one point. Then it exploded into—call it "dust"—which coalesced into the elements and molecules, which, in turn, coalesced into stars and planets, into primordial soup that, on earth at least, generated life, with random evolution doing the rest.

What Pullman does is glorify and mystify this "dust." He believes that material particles alone can do all of this. How wonderful they must be. They have evolved into love and consciousness. Such dust is deserving of honor as the source of all things, deserving, too, of worship. Classic paganism is essentially nature worship. Pagans worship the sun, and they are also willing to worship personifications of the sun, such as Apollo the sun god. They are similar to atheists in assuming that nature is all there is. Pullman's fantasy manages to mythologize materialism, thus making it enchanting.

> The irony is that Pullman is doing what atheists have always criticized religious people for doing, replacing reason with imagination, indulging in wish-fulfillment and escapism.

Here is how Pullman writes about death. The atheistic view of that subject, of course, lacks imaginative appeal: that the body is all we are; that when we die, we are put in a coffin, buried in the ground, where we rot away, becoming food for worms, our consciousness swallowed up by black nothingness.

That prospect is too horrible for most people to contemplate. The notion that we are more than our physical bodies, that our identity is a spiritual one that lasts beyond this life and beyond the grave, with an eternal life in heaven or in hell, resonates far more with the human imagination. But notice how Pullman describes death as a dissolution, while at the same time making it seem like a good thing:

> When you go out of here, all the particles that make you up will loosen and float apart, just like your daemons did. If you've seen people dying, you know what that looks like. But your daemons aren't just nothing now; they're part of everything. All the atoms that were them, they've gone into the air and the wind and the trees and the earth and all the living things. They'll never vanish. They're just part of everything. And that's exactly what'll happen to you, I swear to you, I promise on my honor. You'll drift apart, it's true, but you'll be out in the open, part of everything alive again.[22]

"Dust to dust," agrees the Christian burial service. "For you are dust, and to dust you shall return" (Gen. 3:19). We are indeed embodied, and there will come a time when we will rise again with our bodies. But the way Pullman tells it, when our bodies break up into their constituent carbon, hydrogen, and oxygen atoms, it will be great. We will fly around in the air. We will become a part of trees. We will be part of all kinds of living things. So we will, in a sense, have a life after death, even though—rather, because—we rot.

We will not have a consciousness to enjoy all this freedom, but, still, the idea has great imaginative appeal. The nothingness of death becomes similar to the "nothingness" of Eastern religions, in which we become one with the universe. Becoming one with the universe is a rather good description of what it means to be dead.

In *The Amber Spyglass*, Will cuts into the world of the dead, where the Authority puts those who have died. This world of the dead is a conflation of heaven and hell, in which some are tormented forever (showing God's cruelty) and others exist in a gray, ghostlike condition in utter boredom. Will, defying the Authority, uses the subtle knife to cut out a window out of this hell and allows the captive spirits to escape, leading them to freedom. As soon as they get into the regular world, these dead people just dissolve:

> The first ghost to leave the world of the dead was Roger. He took a step forward, and turned to look back at Lyra, and laughed in surprise as he found himself turning into the night, the starlight, the air ... and then he was gone, leaving behind such a vivid little burst of happiness that Will was reminded of the bubbles in a glass of champagne.[23]

The atheistic view of death is presented as so much *better* than the religious notion of an afterlife. Dissolving into dust is a matter for laughter that feels like a "burst of happiness."

Pullman makes atheism heroic and exciting, in contrast to the drab and cowardly conformity of faith. He makes atheism seem moral, the force for kindness and acceptance, over against the cruelty and intolerance of God and his followers. He makes atheism into a worldview full of mystery and mysticism. This is a significant advance in the history of atheism. Already, atheistic publications are hailing *His Dark Materials* in excited, even giddy terms. Pullman's trilogy may even become the atheists' equivalent of the Bible, a source for instruction, inspiration, and evangelism.

Of course, the fact that something has imaginative appeal does not make it true. The question is, for example, is there life after death? Are heaven and hell real, and if so, how can we escape the latter and enjoy the former? Is there a God, or not? If there is, what is he like and what is his disposition toward us?

The irony is that Pullman is doing what atheists have always criticized religious people for doing, replacing reason with imagination, indulging in wish-fulfillment and escapism. Pullman surely knows that if the physical body is all there is, and if the body dissolves into its constituent chemicals, there can be no consciousness, nothing to feel "happiness" in merging with a blade of grass or with the air, nothing to "be alive" in becoming a part of the worms that eat us and the birds that eat them.

Pullman believes that just because there is no God does not mean that we should be immoral. What is the basis for morality? The "dust," which evolved into people who can have such noble ideals. But the old materialist challenge should apply to the materialist as well: "Show me a moral ideal. Such ideals are not material; what is, does not necessarily reflect what should be." What the classic materialists took for evidence that morality does not exist, Christians—particularly C. S. Lewis—took for evidence that the spiritual realm does exist.[24]

But Pullman wants to have it both ways. If evolution from dust is all we are, why should we be "kind," as he exhorts us in the last words of the trilogy? Does not evolution function by the survival of the fittest, by conflict in which the strong prey on the weak? Where is kindness in nature? In criticizing the cruelty of his fictional god and the corruption of his fictional church, isn't Pullman drawing on moral standards from a realm beyond the dust, grounded in the true God, beyond space and time, who is truly righteous and truly loving?

Pullman has made atheism at least as irrational as the old atheists charged Christianity as being. Christians have long insisted that atheism is a religion, which most atheists have denied. But Pullman agrees that it is a religion, adding the myth and the mystification that any religion, however false, really needs to meet the spiritual needs of its followers.

Pullman's theological contribution to atheism is to make it attractive to this postmodernist age, which assumes that truth is as relative as Pullman's various worlds and which rejects reason altogether. Though in Lyra's world, Christianity has no Reformation, Pullman may be the atheists' Luther, sparking a reformation of atheism that will make it culturally palatable again.

> Legions of adolescents and teenagers, who are the biggest fans of *His Dark Materials*, will grow up in the true faith of unbelief, their religious needs met—without unpleasant demands—in a faith without God.

Meanwhile, the legions of adolescents and teenagers who are the biggest fans of *His Dark Materials* will grow up in the true faith of unbelief, their religious needs met—without unpleasant demands—in a faith without God.

C. S. Lewis predicted that this apostasy would happen. The union of materialism and spirituality, atheism and fantasy, is what Screwtape, Lewis's fictitious Devil, projected as "the perfect work" of demonic deception:

> "If once we can produce our perfect work—the Materialist Magician, the man, not using, but veritably worshipping what he vaguely calls 'Forces' while denying the existence of 'Spirits'—then the end of the war will be in sight."[25]

The figure of the Materialist Magician occurs other times in Lewis's fiction. He is a scientist who cultivates the occult in Lewis's science-fiction novel *That Hideous Strength*. Another materialist magician is Uncle Andrew in *The Magician's Nephew* ... the man who brought sin into Narnia.

CHAPTER 11

THE LION AND THE SENILE OLD MAN

One wonders what C. S. Lewis would say about Philip Pullman, someone who had declared out-and-out war on Narnia and all that it represents. Actually, Lewis would probably have liked parts of *His Dark Materials*. He was a remarkably fair-minded and generous critic. Lewis praised and defended Percy Bysshe Shelley for the flights of his imagination, even when the poet had fallen out of favor and even though he was an atheist. Conversely, Lewis savaged the poetry of T. S. Eliot for its modernist realism and for its bleak experimental verse, even though Eliot was a fellow Christian (which Lewis said was far more important in unifying them than their differences in literary taste).[1] *His Dark Materials* is a creative, imaginative fantasy that sends the mind reeling, and Lewis would have appreciated that fact.

But we do know what Lewis would say about the central conceit of Pullman's fantasy, his appropriation of Milton, and his taking the side of the rebel angels. Lewis's day job, when he was not writing Christian apologetics or imaginative fiction, was being a highly respected literary scholar on the faculty of Oxford and then Cambridge. His specialty was Medieval and Renaissance Literature, and he was an expert on the poetry of John Milton, one of his favorite writers. In *A Preface to Paradise Lost*, a book that to this day is one of the best discussions of Milton's epic, Lewis discusses the fad then current of interpreting God as the villain of the poem and Satan as the hero.

> It was the Gnostics the apostle John refuted in his gospel, emphasizing that "the Word became flesh" (John 1:14).

Milton Twisting

Pullman uses Milton, but an even stronger influence would be William Blake, the brilliant but eccentric poet of the eighteenth century who defied the Enlightenment Age of Reason with his visionary poetry and illustrations. Blake was associated with the Swedenborgians, a mystical cult, who followed not only the tenets but the mythology of Gnosticism.[2]

According to the Gnostic myths, which the early church battled, the God of the Old Testament was evil. After all, he created the world—or seemed to—and the Gnostics believed this ordinary world is the realm of illusion. He also seemed, to the Gnostics' way of thinking, cruel and judgmental. The

Serpent, though, in promising Adam and Eve knowledge, or *gnosis*, was the liberator. Whereas God the Father was considered oppressive, Jesus was considered nice. More of the Serpent's party, this Jesus, the Gnostics believed, was a spiritual emanation. He was emphatically *not* the incarnation of God, nor did he have a genuinely physical body, nor did he die on the cross, nor did he rise physically from the dead. It was the Gnostics the apostle John refuted in his gospel, emphasizing that "the Word became flesh" (John 1:14), and in his epistles, in which he gives as a sign of the Antichrist the denial that Jesus Christ came in the flesh (1 John 4:2; 2 John 1:7).

Blake wrote his own visionary epics, one of which was titled *Milton*, in which he developed his own story of the creation, fall, and redemption of mankind. Here he followed the Gnostic line, with Jehovah, the God of the Old Testament, being the negative force and the rebel angel being the positive energy. It was Blake who first popularized the revisionist reading of Milton when he said that "Milton was of the Devil's party without knowing it."[3] In doing so, he inspired a line of critics, who achieved special prominence in the twentieth century and who attempted to turn *Paradise Lost* upside down.

Notice that once again we have Gnosticism, the ancient heresy that is making a comeback in popular culture and is, arguably, the religion—even in this atheistic guise—that may prove to be Christianity's chief competitor in the twenty-first century.[4] That is the link between *The Da Vinci Code* and *His Dark Materials*.

One factor in the inverted reading of *Paradise Lost* is critics' puzzlement that Milton himself was a revolutionary, an activist with the Puritans who overthrew the English monarchy and executed King Charles I. (This happened in 1649, so that

England was governed as a republic until the restoration of the monarchy in 1660 when Charles II took the throne.) Milton was a rebel against the monarchy of England. Satan is a rebel against the monarchy of heaven. Isn't there a parallel here? Being a Puritan, Milton would not have consciously been on Satan's side, some critics reason, but *subconsciously* he must have been.

Lewis explains that there is no contradiction whatsoever, that modern readers are confused because they do not understand the seventeenth-century view of hierarchy. After explaining the concept from Aristotle through the Middle Ages and the Renaissance, he concludes:

> If once the conception of Hierarchy is fully grasped, we see that order can be destroyed in two ways: (1) By ruling or obeying natural equals, that is by Tyranny or Servility. (2) By failing to obey a natural superior or to rule a natural inferior—that is, by Rebellion or Remissness.... The idea, therefore, that there is any logical inconsistency, or even any emotional disharmony, in asserting the monarchy of God and rejecting the monarchy of Charles II is a confusion. We must first inquire whether Charles II is, or is not, our natural superior. For if he is not, rebellion against him would not be departure from the hierarchical principle, but an assertion of it; we should obey God and disobey Charles for one and the same reason—just as even a modern man might obey the law and refuse to obey a gangster for one and the same reason.[5]

Pullman rejects *all* hierarchy, but he thinks of hierarchy only in Lewis's sense number two. Pullman thinks there should be no natural superiors (not even, say, the authority that a parent has over a child?) and so values rebellion.

Milton—and Lewis—would disagree. But for them, tyranny is just as much a violation of hierarchy as rebellion. Tyranny, in which a mere human being imposes his will on people who are actually his equals, is a *violation* of God's order. Milton, Lewis, the Puritans, and all Christians would agree that the evil deeds of Pullman's villains—including those identified with the church and including the bogus "Authority" himself—are wrong. But Pullman refuses to acknowledge any legitimate authority, by which the false authorities can be judged.

> Tyranny, in which a mere human being imposes his will on people who are actually his equals, is a violation of God's order.

Another factor that has made the inverted reading of *Paradise Lost* plausible to some readers is that the *character* of Satan in Milton's poem is one of the greatest literary creations in world literature. The way Milton portrays him is unforgettable, having him speak lines that are unsurpassed in their descriptions of ego, malice, and pride. "Better to reign in Hell than serve in Heaven."[6] What an expression of defiance, ambition, and perversity! And Milton puts hundreds of lines like these into the mouth of his character.

Milton's character of God, on the other hand, is not nearly so poetically effective. God the Father speaks in the voice of calm reason and absolute authority, without the poetic "personality" of his adversary. Sometimes Milton rises to the occasion—as when he describes the Father as "dark with excessive bright"[7] (that is, his light is so bright that we cannot gaze on him, just as all we see is darkness when we try to stare into the sun). Also, Milton's portrayal of the Son of God is much better. But most readers agree that Milton's rendition of the Deity does not work as well as his rendition of Satan.

Lewis also agrees; but, he says, there is good reason. It is always easier for an author to write about a bad character than a good character. Because of our fallen nature, we can understand sin better than we can understand virtue.

> To make a character worse than oneself it is only necessary to release imaginatively from control some of the bad passions which, in real life, are always straining at the leash; the Satan, the Iago, the Becky Sharp, within each of us, is always there and only too ready … to come out and have in our books that holiday we try to deny them in our lives.[8]

> The Satan in Milton enables him to draw the character well just as the Satan in us enables us to receive it.[9]

Conversely, our fallenness is why God, as a literary character, is largely outside our imaginative grasp.

Lewis goes on in *A Preface to Paradise Lost* to show that while we might be impressed with the literary character of Satan, as a successful work of art, we would not actually admire him or people like him in real life. Lewis unpacks the absurdities that Satan is caught up in, his "inaccuracy" and his "nonsense." In a memorable passage, Lewis shows how, in Milton's poem, Satan—like all egotistical boors—always brings the subject back to himself: "He meets Sin—and states his position. He sees the Sun; it makes him think of his own position. He spies on the human lovers; and states his position. In Book IX he journeys round the whole earth; it reminds him of his own position."[10]

Though much of the misinterpretation of *Paradise Lost* is due to simple misreading, something Lewis the literary historian and critic can help correct, there is also sometimes a deeper problem. Lewis notes that one of his fellow critics understands Milton quite well. But "he sees and hates the very same that I see and love."[11] There is a fundamental conflict in worldviews. "The adverse criticism of Milton is not so much a literary phenomenon as the shadow cast upon literature by revolutionary politics, antinomian ethics, and the worship of Man by Man."[12]

In a post-Christian era, of course, a Christian poem is likely to be either incomprehensible or willfully misinterpreted. "Many of those who say they dislike Milton's God," observes Lewis, "only mean that they dislike God."[13]

Perhaps more so than in Lewis's time, Satan's values—which Milton in his poem is criticizing—have become the values of people today. Many contemporary readers admire Satan because they, too, would rather reign in hell than serve in heaven. They share Satan's preoccupation with his own sweet self. They share his pride and his desire to be God, along with his absurdity and his despair.

Lewis's description of Satan sounds familiar: "What we see in Satan is the horrible co-existence of a subtle and incessant intellectual activity with an incapacity to understand anything."[14] Brilliant minds that have nothing in them. A powerful imagination that misses its own points. This description could apply to the legions of contemporary intellectuals and artists, the professors of our elite universities and their students, but also more ordinary and typical citizens of the postmodern world. But this mind-set has consequences. "To admire Satan," Lewis writes, "is to give one's vote not only for a world of misery, but also for a world of lies and propaganda, of wishful thinking, of incessant autobiography."[15]

> The God who has revealed himself to us and who actively works in our lives is nothing like Pullman's dried-up old man. He is much more like a certain Lion.

The Old Man and the Lion

The British Christian author Mark Greene, a critic of Pullman's books, tells how he first learned about them, and, in doing so, through the insight of a child, neatly puts them in their place:

> I first encountered these stories through the enthusiasm of my then 12-year-old god-daughter who admired the brilliance of Pullman's adventure but was able to

dismiss his anti-Christian propaganda with the non-chalance of a donkey flicking away a fly. "Pullman's God," she said, "is nothing like the God I worship."[16]

Precisely. Pullman is trying to discredit the God of Christianity, but he misses his target. Not that his caricatures may not be harmful to those on the verge of abandoning their faith or to those who refuse to take Christianity seriously (the very sort that Lewis is so helpful in winning over). But to those who know God, who have come to know him not as an abstract idea but personally through his Son, Jesus Christ, Pullman's diatribes have no effect. The God we know is just not like that doddering, senile, mean old man. He is not just our "Authority"; he is our Savior. He is no distant, detached being in a crystal litter; he has become incarnate and has offered himself as our sacrifice. He is not oppressive; he has given us freedom. The God who has revealed himself to us and who actively works in our lives is nothing like Pullman's dried-up old man. He is much more like a certain Lion.

Pullman's attacks on the church can also be easily flicked away. Is the actual church really so oppressive? When was the last time your congregation planned an inquisition? Certainly, there are shameful chapters in the history of the church. But are these aberrations or the norm? As for the Inquisition, its major victims were Protestants, Jewish converts to Christianity, and Catholics who had come to know the gospel as uncovered by the Reformation. How can the Inquisition be used to discredit the faith of those it persecuted?

His charge that Christianity has been a force for repression—that "every advance in human life, every scrap of knowledge and wisdom and decency we have has been torn by one side from the teeth of the other. Every little increase in human freedom has been fought over ferociously between those who want us to know more and be wiser and stronger, and those who want us to obey and be humble and submit"[17]—is equally preposterous. Consider the countries in the world today that enjoy political freedom, technological advances, and social progress. Then consider those that do not. Which group of countries was shaped by Christianity?

The truth is, Christianity always brings freedom and progress into a society, and the more biblical the Christianity, the more freedom and progress can be found. This fact is thoroughly demonstrated in Stanton Evans' book *The Theme Is Freedom*,[18] which shows that even in the Middle Ages, it was Christianity that was insisting on human rights and on mitigating the oppressiveness of the old pagan cultures. Evans describes what Pullman here believes—that the regressive power of Christianity was challenged by liberation movements such as the Renaissance and the Enlightenment—as a myth. It was the humanism of the Renaissance that invented the concept of the absolute monarch. It was the Enlightenment that gave us the Reign of Terror, Napoleonic dictatorship, and the dialectical materialism that would bear fruit in Soviet Communism.

How was it that Milton and his fellow Puritans so loved freedom that they overthrew the British king? They arguably went overboard in their zeal. How was it that their descendants, exiled from England for their anti-monarchical religion, started the American Revolution and established a free republic? These rebels were mostly Calvinists, holding the creed Pullman associates the most with cruelty and oppression. Were they all, as Pullman thinks of Milton, on the rebel angels' side unawares? Or is Pullman failing to understand what they were all about?

Pullman and his fellow atheists, and perhaps today's secularist culture as a whole, do not understand Milton or his fellow Puritans or C. S. Lewis or Christians, in general. Pullman and company think Christianity is just about rules and morality and legalism, whereas instead Christianity is precisely about *liberation*. They think that *we think* that God is an old, gray-bearded man in the sky, who looks down from the clouds to punish people when they do wrong. They do not realize—or perhaps they have never been told—that what makes Christianity distinct from every other religion is not the moral law (all religions, and even, as Pullman insists, atheists can believe in morality) but the gospel. That is, it is not about obedience but about forgiveness when we are not obedient. Not about God's punishment, but his grace.

> Pullman and company think Christianity is just about rules and morality and legalism, whereas instead Christianity is precisely about liberation.

Christianity is about *Christ*. Ours is an *incarnate* God. He is Jesus Christ. (Interestingly, those who believe in history as the liberation from superstitious oppression tend to see Jesus as someone on the liberation side, who was then deified by the oppressive side. They say they like Jesus. *But he is the*

Christian's God.) "Whoever has seen me," said Jesus, "has seen the Father" (John 14:9).

So we cannot think of God as the decrepit old man who breaks apart into nothingness when he gets exposed to the air. God is so much more complicated than that simple-minded stereotype. We believe in the Trinity, that God is Father, Son, and Holy Spirit, a union of three distinct persons so complete that we can say that "God is love" (1 John 4:8). Not cruelty, *love*.

To go back to Narnia, notice that *The Lion, the Witch and the Wardrobe* is, like Pullman's novels, about a rebellion. The beavers and Tumnus are, at first, part of an underground movement against the White Witch and her secret police. Aslan comes to overthrow her.

Could Pullman invert Lewis's story, as he does Milton's, and argue that the witch is on the right side, boldly rebelling against an evil, oppressive Lion? That would be hard to manage. It is the witch who is the oppressive one, just as Milton's Satan becomes an utterly ruthless tyrant to his subjects.

> Aslan is not a tame lion, nor is the One he symbolizes less than a mystery.

Though Pullman and company think *they* are the rebels, of course, they actually represent the intellectual and cultural establishment today. They are the ones getting Whitbread Prizes and other accolades. It is their materialism that is taught in most schools and universities, while Christianity—far from being powerful—is pushed out to the margins, becoming almost invisible to the culture as a whole. For Pullman and his followers to congratulate themselves on rebelling against the establishment is ludicrous, since *they* are the establishment.

So Christians are the ultimate rebels against those great powers that enslave the world: sin, death, and the Devil. "Everyone who commits sin is a slave to sin," says Jesus. "So if the Son sets you free, you will be free indeed" (John 8:34, 36).

As an alternative to Pullman's shriveled-up old deity, Lewis gives us the Lion. As we have seen, the figure of Aslan expresses the complex range of qualities that we know of God through his incarnation in Christ: He is strong and ferocious, yet he can be gentle; frightening his enemies, yet romping with children like a kitten. He is sovereign, yet he subjects himself to his own creation. He is the judge of the world, but he gives up his life to save sinners. He can be known intimately, and yet can never be fully comprehended. Aslan is not a tame lion, nor is the One he symbolizes less than a mystery.

Pullman gets the title, *His Dark Materials*, from a passage in *Paradise Lost*, which he quotes in the front of the first book as the epigraph to the series. In the context of the poem, Satan is getting ready to fly to the new world God has made, where he will get revenge upon God, not by an inevitably futile attempt to defeat in battle One who is almighty, but by seducing to his party these new creatures that God loves. Before setting out, Satan peers into the outer space that he must travel through to get to earth, conceived by Milton as a chaos of matter lacking form:

> Into this wild abyss,
> The womb of nature and perhaps her grave,
> Of neither sea, nor shore, nor air, nor fire,
> But all these in their pregnant causes mixed

Confusedly, and which thus must ever fight,
Unless the almighty maker them ordain
His dark materials to create more worlds,
Into this wild abyss the wary fiend
Stood on the brink of hell and looked a while,
Pondering his voyage.[19]

Pullman exalts both the chaos and the "dark materials," described here as the raw material from which everything is made, which in Pullman's imagination becomes the "dust" that has evolved to love and consciousness. For Milton, though, the chaos can be given form by "the almighty maker." Fantasy writers like "to create more worlds." So does God. Both in worlds of the imagination and in worlds of reality, the "dark materials" are "his."

CHAPTER 12

CONCLUSION

The Gospel through Stories

C. S. Lewis wrote a number of books designed to make the case that Christianity and its teachings are true. *Mere Christianity, The Problem of Pain, Miracles,* and other writings show that there are good reasons to believe in Jesus Christ.

Although, strictly speaking, it is probably impossible to reason anyone into the faith—the Holy Spirit has to be at work—still, many people have said that these books played an important role in forming their Christian faith and convictions. Lewis's works have played a role not only in bringing people to faith, but in keeping Christians in their faith in the face of the opposition.

It is not only his nonfiction, though, that does this; his fiction does as well.

Lewis's works of apologetics and popular theology are extraordinarily effective in conveying the truths of Christianity in an appealing and persuasive way. They speak to thoughtful, intelligent readers—a group some churches, in their anti-intellectualism, tragically ignore—and to those with a mind-set that demands logic and evidence before they will accept a belief or a set of beliefs.

His fiction, though, also effectively conveys the truths of the gospel in an appealing and persuasive way. Just as his nonfiction works through reason, his fiction works through imagination. His stories speak to another group that some churches—in their narrow indifference to beauty and creativity—sometimes ignore. (Some people, of course, including many who as children were raised in the church, are *both* thoughtful *and* imaginative and have been ignored by their churches for both reasons.) Lewis's fiction also addresses those whose beliefs are formed not by cold rationalism, but by a yearning for mystery.

> Lewis's fiction also addresses those whose beliefs are formed not by cold rationalism, but by a yearning for mystery.

Evangelizing the Modernists

During Lewis's lifetime Christianity was under attack from many different sides, a situation that has not changed but may have gotten worse. The modernists, heirs to the Age of Reason, refuse to believe anything that cannot be proven logically. They consider Christianity to be nothing more than irrational superstition, a matter of inner, subjective feelings rather than any kind of truth about what exists in the real world. Since religious ideas cannot be proven scientifically—"Show me God, moral absolutes, or heaven," they say—such concepts cannot claim to be true.

This view has been prominent in universities and among the intellectual elite for more than a century. College students whose faith is challenged by their professors along these lines sometimes cannot answer them. Sometimes, in their desire to be "intellectually respectable"—usually coupled with a moral temptation—people give in to this way of thinking, stop going to church, and abandon their faith.

Lewis has responded to such assaults on Christianity in their own terms. To those who live in the Age of Reason, he has shown that Christianity *is* reasonable. To those who will not take anything seriously unless it can be demonstrated with logic, he demonstrates Christianity with logic.

Not that there is a rigid, logical proof of Christianity's beliefs that will convince everyone. The human mind is fallen along with the human will, and sin makes people "blind" to spiritual truths (Luke 6:39; 2 Cor. 4:4). Again, the Holy Spirit brings people to faith, as Jesus gives sight to the blind, both physically as he did in Judea (John 9:25) and spiritually as he did with John Newton, the author of "Amazing Grace."

What Lewis does in books like *Mere Christianity* is not so much to prove Christianity; rather he simply addresses the logical

> What Lewis does in books like *Mere Christianity* is not so much to prove Christianity but rather to address the logical mind.

mind. His explanations of the objective moral law and of the Trinity "make sense." He talks about Christianity in a way thoughtful people can relate to, showing that not only can it stand up to intense scrutiny but that it also makes better sense than the humanly devised philosophies thoughtful people tend to create for themselves. Above all, he clarifies the issues, as for example in that passage echoed by the Professor, in which he says that Lucy must have been either lying, mad, or telling the truth about Narnia (p. 45). Lewis's meaning is, of course, that when Jesus said he was the Son of God, either he was a liar, a madman, or who he claimed to be.

Some unbelievers today do maintain that Jesus is a liar, that the authors of the New Testament were not recording what actually happened but were making it up for various reasons. (But as Lewis, in another example of how he keeps afflicting the critics of Christianity with the facts, points out, as a literary historian, if these accounts are not straight history as their style suggests, they must be a type of prose fiction that would not be invented for seventeen hundred years.[1]) Yet people still make the claim that the Bible stories are fiction, even though Lewis makes it harder for them to do so credibly.

Other unbelievers do maintain that Jesus is a madman, a delusional prophet who imagined that the world was coming to an end. Ironically, that is the position of many liberal theologians in the church, a group that Lewis skewers regularly.

To truly believe and confess that Jesus is the Son of God requires a revelation from God. It even did so for Peter, Jesus' disciple, someone who *did* see Jesus and his miracles for himself in an empirical way:

> Now when Jesus came into the district of Caesarea Philippi, he asked his disciples, "Who do people say that the Son of Man is?" And they said, "Some say John the Baptist, others say Elijah, and others Jeremiah or one of the prophets." He said to them, "But who do you say that I am?" Simon Peter replied, "You are the Christ, the Son of the living God." And Jesus answered him, "Blessed are you, Simon Bar-Jonah! For flesh and blood has not revealed this to you, but my Father who is in heaven." (Matt. 16:13–17)

What Lewis is doing in posing those three alternatives is to eliminate the fuzzy thinking that so often gets in the way of every kind of truth, including divine truth. He explains Christian beliefs—which are often so muddled that they are easy targets for skeptics—with great clarity, so that their true magnitude comes shining through. In other words, Lewis is an effective communicator to people of his time and ours, particularly to thoughtful and educated people who often get short shrift from many churches. What he does is present the truth of Christ in his own words in a language that modernists can understand, a presentation of the Word that the Holy Spirit can then use to engender faith in the hearts of his readers.

Evangelizing the Postmodernists

But though Lewis is effective in communicating the Christian faith to modernists, with their fixation on human reason, beginning in his lifetime but accelerating into dominance

> Whereas modernists reject Christianity because it cannot be objectively verified, postmodernists reject Christianity because it is *too* objective and because it insists *too much* on being true.

today is a different group of critics of Christianity, the postmodernists.[2] They reject the claims of objective reason, insisting that truth is nothing more than an individual or cultural construction. "Truth is relative," they say. "All truth claims and meaning systems are, in effect, fictions."

Whereas modernists reject Christianity because it cannot be objectively verified, postmodernists reject Christianity because it is *too* objective and because it insists *too much* on being true. "Christianity has all of these objective doctrines that it insists on," postmodernists complain. "Christians say that theirs is the only true religion, that Jesus is the only way to salvation. Why can't they just let everybody choose for themselves what works for them? Why can't they affirm that all religions are equally valid? Religion needs to be an interior, completely private choice, something that enables a person to create his or her own meaning. Someone's personal religion may be true for that person, but it cannot be valid for everybody else."

It is said that while modernists respond best to arguments, postmodernists respond best to stories. A convinced postmodernist believes that practically everything—even an argument—is a "constructed" narrative, that is, a work of fiction.

Those who are not convinced postmodernists, but who have only soaked up their antirationalism from the culture, also tend to be unfazed by arguments, however sound, but they often respond powerfully to stories.[3]

Those who believe that religion is a personal construction may think that such beliefs are relative, but they are often willing to listen to other people's beliefs, especially when they are personalized, when they are presented as a personal *story*. This is often the opening Christians need, remembering that postmodern listeners will respond better to an account of how the speaker came to faith and what Christ has done in his or her life than to any kind of abstract argument.

But this can be a forum for proclaiming the gospel, for putting out the Word of God in a way that the Holy Spirit can use to create faith in the hearts of even the most avid of relativists (Rom. 10:14–17). And it is possible, to those used to thinking in terms of narratives, to tell true stories. Or to tell fictional stories that nevertheless convey truth.

Just as C. S. Lewis's nonfiction works are effective in reaching modernists by showing reasons to believe in Christian doctrine, his fictional works are effective in reaching postmodernists by telling the Christian *story*. Lewis addresses his readers' intellect with Christian truth in his nonfiction, and he addresses his readers' imagination with Christian truth in his fiction.

The Chronicles of Narnia, his science-fiction trilogy, *The Great Divorce*, and *The Screwtape Letters* relate objective Christian doctrine to tangible, concrete life. They also appeal to another quality of postmodernists, their desire for mystery. Postmodernists not only do not have to have logical reasons to believe in something, they tend to prefer beliefs that do not have a logical reason. This is why they prefer "spirituality" to "religion," embracing the mystical rather than the rational. This tendency can get postmodernists into trouble, leading them into flying saucer cults and New Age occultism. Those who have no concept of truth in their religion can be manipulated into believing just about anything, as long as it appeals to their desires and gives personal meaning to their lives.

One way Christianity can answer is to recover its own rich "spirituality," and the "mysteries" of salvation—the incarnation, the atonement, the resurrection, and the life of the redeemed—which no one can fully grasp by human reason. Nor could we have ever just dreamed up or constructed for ourselves such mind-blowing truths. Rather, they come from outside ourselves, by revelation of the Holy Spirit in God's Word, which puts them into a completely different category from both modernism with its reason and postmodernism with its antireason.

> I used to give copies of *Mere Christianity* to my non-Christian friends. I have started instead to have them read his fiction, including *The Lion, the Witch and the Wardrobe.*

The Lion, the Witch and the Wardrobe, like Lewis's other fiction, evokes these mysteries and brings back the true mystery inherent in teachings that to many people have become old hat. He tells God's story in a way, as we have seen, to get past "watchful dragons."

I used to give copies of *Mere Christianity* to my non-Christian friends. At one time, the book left a strong impression (and sometimes still does for some people, the modernists and those who still use their minds). But lately, I have been frustrated by the way they say how glad they are that Lewis has the beliefs that he does, but that they have their own truths. His logical handling of Christianity does not get through to them. For people like that, I have them read Lewis's fiction, including *The Lion, the Witch and the Wardrobe*.

How Atheists Now Must Evangelize

It is significant that atheists are having to adjust their argumentation in the same way that Christians are. In the modernist era, materialists were dead set against any kind of fantasy. They lambasted not just Christians but romantics—anyone who persisted in any kind of idealism or mystification, thus avoiding the hard, cold facts that are all there is in a Godless, disenchanted reality.

In the past, the modernist, materialistic, rationalistic atheists would never have dreamed of writing a fantasy, a form they ridiculed. Instead, they wrote depressing realistic novels. They showed idealistic romantics destroyed by the indifferent determinism of nature. They showed upright moral people brought down by their true animal instincts. They showed naïve religious folk "waking up" to the true absurdity of life.

Ironically, while that approach worked well in the late 1800s and through much of the 1900s in addressing the "modern mind," those novels—though sometimes still being written and read—seem too depressing to appeal to people today. More than that, their worldview seems too depressing.

Of course, the fact that a worldview is depressing is no evidence that it is not true. But postmodernists care little for reason and *do* choose their beliefs according to what appeals to them, according to whether they "like it" or not. To them, materialism is just too bleak, and they would much rather embrace some kind of cool paganism, or construct their own religion according to their personal tastes and desires.

So now we have an atheist, Philip Pullman, writing a fantasy in which he is *mystifying* atheism. As we have seen, he agrees completely with the old materialists that the universe is nothing but dust, but he turns it into *magic* dust. It is still the same old dust, but he emphasizes what to Christians makes materialism seem so unlikely and unconvincing: the marvel that this dust is able to evolve into human beings, with all of their consciousness, love, morality, and ideals.

The old materialists stressed determinism, the view that we are all controlled by inexorable natural laws. The novelist Thomas Hardy was always showing his characters being swept away by forces—such as their animal instincts—that they could not control. Now, the fantasist Philip Pullman stresses instead the importance of *freedom*. For Hardy, it was the Christians who held to the naïve belief that human beings possess freedom and the moral responsibility that goes with it, views that he tried to discredit in his novels. For Pullman, it is the Christians who oppose freedom, insisting as they do on moral responsibility, whereas atheists

> Even nonbelievers are having to win people over by means of stories.

offer freedom to do as one likes (though, strangely, going on to urge moral responsibility).

So even nonbelievers are having to win people over by means of stories. Of course, far more influential than *His Dark Materials* are the stories in movies and on television, the narratives of lust and glamour and hedonism that seem to be seducing the whole culture into a depraved kind of unbelief. And however much they masquerade as what is possible in real life, these stories too are fantasies.

The Christian Story

In this climate, Christian stories are all the more important. In a profound way, the very forms of narrative, fiction, and fantasy belong to Christians.

As we have seen, fantasy—high fantasy, and, if we can say so, true fantasy—is a great contribution of the distinctly Christian literary tradition.

More than that, as the great literary critic Northrop Frye has shown, the ultimate narrative, the story of all stories that contains and makes possible all the rest, is the Bible.[4] The plot of the Bible has the ultimate beginning (the creation of the universe), conflict (between sin and grace), turning point (the coming of Christ), and finale (the end of time). It embodies tragedy (the tragic fall of sin, the grim realities of suffering, judgment, and the cross) but also comedy (the happy ending of the resurrection and the second coming of our Lord).

The gospel—the good news of salvation through Jesus Christ—is the overarching theme of the Bible, a message that is not just for the evangelism of unbelievers, but for the continual formation of believers who take this Book to heart. And the same can be said of all gospel-bearing stories, including the one about the Deeper Magic from Before the Dawn of Time.

READERS' GUIDE

*For Personal Reflection or
Group Discussion*

Visit www.thesoulofthelion.com for additional powerful teaching and study resources.

Readers' Guide

Introduction: Stealing Past Watchful Dragons

1. Do you sometimes take the Christian truths for granted, to the point of forgetting how amazing they are? What are some "watchful dragons" that give people the impression that Christianity is harsh, drab, or boring?

2. Have you ever experienced what Lewis describes as a "baptism of the imagination"? Has a book, a piece of music, or some other work of art ever affected you the way *Phantastes* affected C. S. Lewis? If not to that extent, has a book ever made things "click" for you, so that you suddenly "got" an important truth?

3. What does the word "imagination" mean? How can the imagination be misused? How can it be used as God intended?

4. Why do so many sermons include *stories*? How can a story that is fiction nevertheless convey truth?

Chapter 1—Narnia: Creation and Sub-creation

1. Besides the wardrobe in *The Chronicles of Narnia*, what else can you think of whose "inside is bigger than its outside"?

2. Explain this statement: "The closest real-world equivalent of going through a wardrobe into a marvelous world is opening a book."

3. How do we, having been created in God's image, imitate God's creativity in our everyday lives?

4. Why do spiritual truths so often find expression in symbols? Give some examples of Christian symbols, and describe what they communicate.

Chapter 2—Sons of Adam and Daughters of Eve: Human Nature in Two Worlds

1. Ah, the carefree, innocent days of childhood! Was your childhood really so carefree? So innocent? What sins do you remember committing against others when you were a child? How did other children sin against you?

2. On the surface, Tumnus and Lucy are having a pleasant tea party, but all the while Tumnus is struggling with a critical moral issue. On the surface, Edmund is just tormenting his little sister, but on the inside, important spiritual issues are being played out. Can you recall a time when routine, day-to-day activities were masking an important interior struggle of your own?

3. Give some more examples of "pure" sin, acts of malice that have no pleasure in them, give the transgressor nothing in return, and are pure "evil for evil's sake."

4. Do you identify more with Lucy or with Edmund? Explain.

5. Have you ever tried to tell people about something wonderful, but they didn't believe you? (For example, witnessing to someone about your faith). Lucy has the same problem with both Peter and Edmund. How are the two boys different in the reasons they do not respond to Lucy's message? How might this scene relate to the different audiences we find when we witness to our faith?

6. The Professor applies "logic" to the children's dilemma and comes up with a surprising conclusion. It parallels C. S. Lewis's classic approach in his apologetic writings, that Jesus must be either a liar, a lunatic, or who he said he was: the Son of God. Consider that argument. Is it persuasive to

you? Is it always going to be persuasive to an unbeliever? Why would any-one, in the face of such logic, still reject Christ?

Chapter 3—The White Witch: The Reign of the Devil

1. What does it mean to be "always winter and never Christmas"? How does this phrase describe the condition of those who do not know Christ?

2. Why is the White Witch described as beautiful?

3. Give some examples of how evil often comes in the guise of something good.

4. How is sin addictive, like Turkish Delight?

5. How can we tell "who is on the right side"?

Chapter 4—Aslan: The Lion of Judah

1. The Bible uses the symbol of a lion to help us grasp certain aspects of the person and work of Christ. Consider some other biblical symbols for Christ: the temple, the lamb, the rock, the stumbling block, the king, the vine. Can you think of others? What does each of these things reveal about Christ?

2. "Aslan is not a tame lion." What does it mean to say that Jesus is not "tame"?

3. When Lucy, Peter, and Susan hear the name "Aslan," they are filled with a sense of joy, beauty, and courage. But Edmund draws back in horror. Today, many people feel uncomfortable hearing the name of Jesus Christ. The very word "Christmas" is avoided in some circles because it has the name Christ in it. Why do you think this happens?

4. When Aslan comes, the snow starts to melt. Unpack the meaning of that symbolism, as it relates to what happens when Christ comes into a person's life.

5. Explain why Aslan is not an "idol."

Chapter 5—The Stone Table: Atonement, Redemption, Justification

1. Edmund's craving for Turkish Delight spoils his enjoyment of wholesome food. Comment on these statements: "Sinful pleasures can ruin the satisfaction we derive from lawful pleasures." "Sinful pleasures soon cease to be pleasures."

2. What does it mean that the witch (that is, the Devil) turns people into stone?

3. Because of what he has done, Edmund belongs to the witch. Because of what we have done, we belong to the Devil. How do you identify with Edmund and his plight?

4. Aslan becomes Edmund's substitute, taking his place on the Stone Table, allowing himself to suffer the death that Edmund deserves. In the same way, Jesus Christ became our substitute: taking our place on the cross, taking the punishment we deserve, suffering our death. How does the account of what Aslan does for Edmund make you realize in a fresh way what Christ has done for you?

5. Explain this statement: "The Deep Magic from the Dawn of Time is the Law; but the Deeper Magic from Before the Dawn of Time is the gospel."

6. Christ died for us, but then he rose from the dead. His new life gives us new life. After Aslan's resurrection, the children "romp" with him. What

does this fact say about the Christian life? How do we "romp" with
Christ?

Chapter 6—The Battle: Sanctification and the Holy Spirit

1. According to C. S. Lewis, a person becoming a Christian is like a statue
   coming to life. How is that analogy true?

2. Those whom the witch has turned to stone come to life when Aslan
   breathes on them. The Bible uses this same imagery in regard to Christ and
   his followers. What can we realize when we think of the Holy Spirit as the
   breath of God? What can we realize about the work of the Holy Spirit when
   we think in terms of our hard hearts turning into living, sensitive flesh?

3. What battles still have to be fought, even after Christ's victory and even
   after we have become Christians? Recall some details from the story that
   give insight into how we Christians can wage this warfare.

4. The children in Narnia are victorious and are crowned as kings and
   queens. But then they must go back into their own world, where they take
   up their ordinary, boring lives again. How is this situation also true of us?

Chapter 7—Coming Back Home: The Spiritual Journey

1. The children have great experiences in Narnia, but when they come back
   to real life, it is as if nothing is changed. Discuss the following passage:

   > Once out of the wardrobe, they are back to normal. Back to
   > World War II. Back to the bad schools. Back to having to grow
   > up. From the outside, say, from the perspective of the tourists
   > they were hiding from if they had walked into the room,
   > nothing external had happened. The children went into the
   > wardrobe and then came out. In the tourists' eyes, nothing
   > has changed. And yet, from the children's point of view, they
   > have undergone something miraculous. Real-life spiritual
   > experiences are like that.

2. Why do you think C. S. Lewis focused on the work of Aslan rather than on Edmund's response? In our evangelism, are we sometimes guilty of focusing on the person's subjective response rather than upon proclaiming the objective work of Christ, a message that itself has the power to create the response of faith?

3. Explain Michael Ward's point that Lewis wanted to create a blank slate "on which his readers could write their own story."

4. Lewis follows the pattern of Shakespeare's fantasies, which move from a "real world" of disorder and disharmony, into a mysterious realm where transformation takes place, and finally back to the "real world" whose order and harmony has been restored. Where else can you see this pattern?

5. The Professor tells the children that they will feel a certain kinship with others who have been to Narnia. He also tells them not to "try" to get back to Narnia, that it will happen apart from their efforts. What do these details tell us about the spiritual life?

Chapter 8—Christianity and Fantasy

1. What do you think about Stan Bohall's contention that since Christianity is not just a matter of abstractions, cognitive knowledge, and rationalistic arguments, evangelism and the teaching of Christian doctrine need to address the imagination? What do you think about his contention that *all* fantasy at least implicitly stirs up issues of Christian truth? Even if you disagree, do you understand what he means by this claim?

2. Why do you think fantasy has become so popular in our culture today?

3. How can "realistic" books distort reality even more than obvious fantasies?

4. The classic Christian author Sir Philip Sidney and the contemporary Christian psychologist William Kirk Kilpatrick both stressed the impor-

tance of stories in moral education. A story can sink deep into the heart because it "teaches by delighting" and inspires its readers to want to emulate the good characters and be repelled by the bad ones. Can you think of examples of how stories played a role in your own moral education? If so, describe them.

5. What is the difference between "good escape" and "bad escape"? Give examples of both.

6. Discuss the following passage:

> Since fantasy grows out of the inner world, its overall danger—when it is dangerous—has to do with the temptation to sink into oneself, to indulge one's sinful imagination (Gen. 8:21), and to wallow in the darkness of our fallen nature. The pseudorealism of a false worldview also shuts us into darkness. Good fantasy, on the other hand, takes us out of ourselves, countering our darkness with at least a glimpse of the external light.

7. How could you use these and the other principles in this chapter to evaluate movies, video games, children's stories, and other fantasies? Take some specific titles of horror movies (*Frankenstein*, *Friday the 13th*), video or computer games (Grand Theft Auto, Myst), books (Anne Rice's vampire novels, Ray Bradbury's science fiction), or other fantasies that you have encountered. (Save *Harry Potter* and *His Dark Materials* for later!) Decide whether each one could be classified as either a "good fantasy" or a "bad fantasy."

Chapter 9—The Lion and the Muggles

1. Do you think there can be such a thing—in fantasy or in reality—as a "good witch," or is this phrase a contradiction in terms?

2. Explain what it means to say that the *Harry Potter* books are "pro-school," while the Narnia books are "anti-school." Which term best describes you?

3. Can a person with a biblical worldview really be a "Muggle"?

4. The heresy of Gnosticism rejects matter, objective truth, and ordinary life in favor of an elite, inner-directed spiritualism. What Gnostic elements can you find in the culture today? How do the Narnia books, in accord with the biblical worldview, reject Gnosticism?

5. Consider the following passage:

> Young Lewis, stuck in his awful schools and imprisoned even more in his materialistic worldview, had always loved fantasy literature. It gave him an escape. But when he picked up George MacDonald's *Phantastes* in that train station, he was introduced to fantasy with a different effect. Before, he said, he had always sought a bright light beyond this world. This time, reading this fantasy, it was as if a bright light were shining on this world.

How does *The Lion, the Witch and the Wardrobe* also shine a bright light on this world?

Chapter 10—The Anti-Lewis and the Anti-Narnia Series

1. Why would an atheist, such as Philip Pullman, have so much angry hatred for *The Chronicles of Narnia*? Why would he consider C. S. Lewis's books so "dangerous"?

2. How does Pullman use fantasy to give the otherwise depressing worldview of atheism and materialism an imaginative and even religious appeal?

3. Why did Lewis warn of the Materialist Magician?

4. Pullman is an evangelist for atheism. How might Christians respond to this kind of "competition"?

Chapter 11—The Lion and the Senile Old Man

1. In *His Dark Materials*, Pullman follows the Gnostics and various Milton critics in projecting a worldview in which God the creator is the villain, Satan is the good guy, and it was a good thing for Adam and Eve to eat the forbidden fruit. What is the attraction of this reinterpretation of the book of Genesis?

2. Non-Christians have a hard time understanding how a Puritan such as Milton, or how contemporary Christian political activists, can be such advocates for freedom. Secularists assume that freedom entails the right to sin. The Bible, though, says that sin is slavery, with Christ making us "free indeed." How do secularists and Christians also have different views of "authority," "morality," "love," and other key human concepts?

3. Lewis says that we tend to find villains in literature more interesting than "good guys," who often come across as relatively bland. But when we encounter those "villainous" characteristics—such as egotism, pride, cynicism, and manipulation—in people we meet in real life, we find them repellent. "Good people," though, are not bland at all, but are usually much more interesting, complex, and pleasant to be around. Can you think of some real-life examples of both "good guys" and "villains" that you have known? Does what Lewis says hold true?

4. Discuss this statement by Lewis: "To admire Satan is to give one's vote not only for a world of misery, but also for a world of lies and propaganda, of wishful thinking, of incessant autobiography." Have you known people to "give their vote" to this kind of world?

5. Mark Greene says, "I first encountered these stories through the enthusiasm of my then 12-year-old god-daughter who admired the brilliance of Pullman's adventure but was able to dismiss his anti-Christian propaganda with the nonchalance of a donkey flicking away a fly. 'Pullman's God,' she said, 'is nothing like the God I worship.'" Can a solid Christian read *His Dark Materials* without being affected by its worldview? Why or why not?

6. Contrast the view of God and of Christianity in *His Dark Materials* with the view of God and of Christianity in *The Lion, the Witch and the Wardrobe*. Which is more accurate? Why do many non-Christians have the negative impression that Pullman does? Are we Christians sometimes to blame for how we come across? How can we show the world what Christianity really is?

Chapter 12—Conclusion: The Gospel through Stories

1. Is it true that churches sometimes neglect the needs of members (particularly young people) who are especially thoughtful and/or imaginative? If so, what could be done to remedy this situation?

2. What can we learn from C. S. Lewis in regard to evangelizing "modernists" who form their beliefs by logic and reason? Why and how must they be taught to open their minds to truths that go beyond their understanding?

3. What can we learn from C. S. Lewis in regard to evangelizing "postmodernists" who believe truth is relative, but yearn for mystery and "spirituality"? Why and how must they be taught to open their minds to objective truth?

4. Sum up what you personally have learned from *The Lion, the Witch and the Wardrobe* and from this book about it. Would you recommend either or both to others? Why or why not?

NOTES

Introduction

1. C. S. Lewis, "It All Began with a Picture," in *Of Other Worlds: Essays and Stories* (New York: Harcourt, Brace & World, 1966), 42.
2. C. S. Lewis, "Sometimes Fairy Stories May Say Best What's to Be Said," in *Of Other Worlds,* 36–37.
3. Ibid., 37.
4. From an unpublished letter, quoted in Donald E. Glover, *C. S. Lewis: The Art of Enchantment* (Athens, OH: Ohio University Press, 1981), 131.
5. C. S. Lewis, *Surprised by Joy: The Shape of My Early Life* (New York: Harcourt Brace Jovanovich, 1956), 178–81. See Elaine Tixier, "Imagination Baptized, or, 'Holiness' in the Chronicles of Narnia," in *The Longing for a Form,* ed. Peter J. Schakel (Kent, OH: Kent State University Press, 1977), 136–58.
6. For Lewis's understanding of metaphor and other figures of speech, see Kath Filmer, "The Polemic Image: The Role of Metaphor and Symbol in the Fiction of C. S. Lewis," in *The Taste of the Pineapple: Essays on C. S. Lewis as Reader, Critic, and Imaginative Writer,* ed. Bruce L. Edwards (Bowling Green, OH: Bowling Green State University Popular Press, 1988), 149–65.
7. The old thinkers, such as Ignatius of Loyola, who talked about the faculties of the mind used the word "memory" to refer to much of what we call imagination.
8. William Kirk Kilpatrick, *Psychological Seduction* (Nashville, TN: Thomas Nelson, 1983), 105–7. See also his title with Gregory Wolfe, Suzanne Wolfe, and Robert Coles, *Books That Build Character: A Guide to Teaching Your Child Moral Values through Stories* (New York: Simon & Schuster, 1994).
9. George Sayer, *Jack: C. S. Lewis and His Times* (San Francisco: Harper and Row, 1988), 192. This is also discussed in Terry W. Glaspey, *Not a Tame Lion: The Spiritual Legacy of C. S. Lewis* (Elkton, MD: Highland Books, 1996), 85.

Chapter 1

1. I am quoting from the Collier paperback edition: C. S. Lewis, *The Lion, the Witch and the Wardrobe* (New York: Collier Books, 1970), 52.
2. C. S. Lewis, *The Last Battle* (New York: Collier Books, 1970), 140.
3. Act 2. scene 2. lines 253–55. The quote continues: "were it not that I have bad dreams."
4. Edmund Spenser, *The Faerie Queene,* Book I, cantos v–vi.
5. C. S. Lewis, *The Last Battle,* 136.
6. Ibid., 140–41.
7. J. R. R. Tolkien, "On Fairy Stories," in *The Monsters and the Critics and Other Essays,* ed. Christopher Tolkien (Boston: Houghton Mifflin, 1984). For Lewis's use of Tolkien's notion of "sub-creation," as well as the differences

in the way the two understood fantasy, see Margaret L. Carter, "Sub-Creation and Lewis's Theory of Literature," in *The Taste of the Pineapple: Essays on C. S. Lewis as Reader, Critic, and Imaginative Writer,* ed. Bruce L. Edwards (Bowling Green, OH: Bowling Green State University Popular Press, 1988), 129–37.

8. C. S. Lewis, *The Allegory of Love* (London: Oxford University Press, 1938), 166.

9. Ibid., 334–60.

10. In a letter dated 29 December 1958, Lewis explained that "if Aslan represented the immaterial Deity in the same way in which Giant Despair [from Spenser's *Faerie Queene*] represents Despair, he would be an allegorical figure. In reality however he is an invention giving an imaginary answer to the question, 'What might Christ become like, if there really were a world like Narnia and if he chose to be incarnate and die and rise again in that world as he actually has done in ours?' This is not allegory at all." *Letters of C. S. Lewis,* ed. W. H. Lewis (New York: Harcourt Brace Jovanovich, 1966), 283. But, as will be seen, Lewis does employ elements of allegory and symbolism in the story's "allegorical core."

Chapter 2

1. George Sayer, *Jack: A Life of C. S. Lewis* (Wheaton, IL: Crossway Books, 1994), 269.

2. Walter Hooper, "Narnia: The Author, the Critics, and the Tale," in *The Longing for a Form: Essays on the Fiction of C. S. Lewis,* ed. Peter J. Schakel (Kent, OH: Kent State University Press, 1977), 106.

3. He turns out to have been the boy Digory, who first enters Narnia, and, in fact, witnesses its creation. The wardrobe was made out of a tree that grew from the seed of an apple that figured prominently in that other story. See C. S. Lewis, *The Magician's Nephew* (New York: Collier Books, 1970), 184–85.

4. C. S. Lewis, *Mere Christianity* (New York: Macmillan, 1952), 55–56. Lewis develops this classic argument further in his essays "Christian Apologetics" and "What Are We to Make of Jesus Christ?" both of which are collected in *God in the Dock: Essays on Theology and Ethics,* ed. Walter Hooper (Grand Rapids, MI: William B. Eerdmans, 1970).

Chapter 3

1. Later in the story, the beavers tell the children that the White Witch is descended from Lilith, Adam's first wife, and a giant (77). This alludes to an old Jewish legend that Adam was at first given a wife made from the dust of the earth, as he was. This Lilith was thus equal to Adam (so that she is often invoked by today's feminists). These two equal—but intrinsically separate—beings could not get along together, though, in their marriage. Lilith ran away and would later consort with demons. Adam was then given Eve, who was made from his rib, so that the two would have a closeness that comes from being "flesh of my [Adam's] flesh." According to the legend, Lilith, now allied with the Devil, became insanely jealous of Eve and of human women, and was blamed for the death of infants. But the beavers do not know what they are talking about. They too must have been repeating a legend. Or, more likely, C. S. Lewis changed his mind. In *The Magician's Nephew,* the White Witch, named Jadis, lives in a completely

different world, named Charn. The materialist magician, Uncle Andrew, is dabbling in the occult and devises an opening into her world. His nephew Digory, who grows up to be the Professor in *The Lion, the Witch and the Wardrobe*, wakes her from her slumbers, whereupon she comes first to earth and then into the just-created Narnia. Here she goes underground for centuries, until at last she manages to slay the true rulers and enslave the inhabitants. Notice that the sin of human beings—particularly, Uncle Andrew—brought sin into Narnia.

Chapter 4

1. See C. S. Lewis, *Surprised by Joy: The Shape of My Early Life* (New York: Harcourt Brace Jovanovich, 1956), 16–17.
2. "The Lion of Judah" connection is found in the classic exposition of the Narnia series by Kathryn Lindskoog, *The Lion of Judah in Never-Never Land: God, Man & Nature in C. S. Lewis's Narnia Tales* (Grand Rapids, MI: William B. Eerdmans, 1973), 50–51. Lewis himself made the connection in a letter answering a young reader's question: He said that he found the name in an edition of *The Arabian Nights*, that it was the "Turkish" word for lion (actually, it is Persian), "And of course I meant the Lion of Judah." C. S. Lewis, *Letters to Children*, ed. Lyle Dorsett and Marjorie Lamp Mead (New York: Macmillan, 1985), 29.
3. Lewis says this is his intention in a letter to an anonymous recipient dated 29 December 1958. See *Letters of C. S. Lewis*, ed. W. H. Lewis (New York: Harcourt, Brace & World, 1966), 283. He also in that letter discusses how his approach in the Narnia stories differs from conventional allegory. He makes the same point in a letter to some fifth-graders, going on to say that while Reepicheep, the mouse in *The Voyage of the Dawn Treader*, does not *represent* anything, whoever seeks heaven will be similar to Reepicheep. C. S. Lewis, *Letters to Children*, 45.
4. Dorothy L. Sayers, *The Mind of the Maker* (New York: Harcourt, Brace, 1941), 90. Discussed in Lindskoog, *The Lion of Judah in Never-Never Land*, 50–51.
5. Lindskoog, *The Lion of Judah in Never-Never Land*, 55.
6. Clyde S. Kilby, *The Christian World of C. S. Lewis* (Grand Rapids, MI: William B. Eerdmans, 1964), 116.
7. Of course, man was created in the "image of God," so a human rendition of the creator might be thought to be more valid. But to say that man was created in the image of God does not mean that God is in the image of man. The text in Genesis 1:26 does not mean that man looks like God, much less that God looks like man. "God is spirit" (John 4:24), and he is beyond any earthly representation (1 Kings 8:27), though the language of the Bible uses tangible comparisons to describe some aspects of him.
8. See the discussion in my book *State of the Arts: From Bezalel to Mapplethorpe* (Wheaton, IL: Crossway, 1991), 54–55.
9. John Kleinig, *Leviticus*, Concordia Commentary (St. Louis: Concordia Publishing House, 2003), 5.
10. For a thorough exposition of these qualities, as explored with Aslan, see Steven P. Mueller, *Not a Tame God: Christ in the Writings of C. S. Lewis* (St. Louis: Concordia Publishing House, 2002), 106–19.
11. Printed in *The Norton Anthology of American Literature*, 3rd ed. (New York: W. W. Norton, 1989), 2: 1276–78.

12. From *The Confessions of St. Augustine.* Quoted in Lindskoog, *The Lion in Never-Never Land,* 16.

13. C. S. Lewis, *Miracles* (New York: Macmillan, 1947), 90–91. Lindskoog cites the same passage in *The Lion of Judah in Never-Never Land,* 18.

14. Martin Luther, "Against the Heavenly Prophets in the Matter of Images and Sacraments" (1535), in *Luther's Works,* ed. Helmut T. Lehmann (Philadelphia: Muhlenberg Press, 1958), chapter 40, 85–86, 99. For further discussion of the Reformers' views on the arts—and how even John Calvin and Ulrich Zwingli were not anti-art—and how these views shaped the art that emerged under their influence, see my book *Painters of Faith: The Spiritual Landscape in Nineteenth-Century America* (Washington, DC: Regnery, 2001), 19–24.

15. C. S. Lewis, *Letters to Children,* 52–53.

16. Ibid., 53.

17. He wrote to a young fan who said that she understood the "hidden" meaning about Jesus and that children usually pick it up, but that adults often do not. C. S. Lewis, *Letters to Children,* 111.

18. C. S. Lewis, *Letters to Children,* 32.

19. C. S. Lewis, *The Voyage of the Dawn Treader* (New York: Collier Books, 1970), 216.

Chapter 5

1. One difference is that Jesus, immediately after he rose from the dead, told Mary Magdalene not to touch him right then (John 20:11–18). The girls in Narnia, though, embrace Aslan.

2. See Peter J. Schakel, *Reading with the Heart: The Way into Narnia* (Grand Rapids, MI: William B. Eerdmans, 1979), 23–29.

3. Ibid., 28.

4. Ibid., 31.

5. Evan K. Gibson, *C. S. Lewis: Spinner of Tales: A Guide to His Fiction* (Grand Rapids, MI: William B. Eerdmans, 1980), 140.

Chapter 6

1. The words are *ruach* in Hebrew and *pneuma* in Greek. See the entries for "spirit," "breath," and "wind" in *Young's Analytical Concordance to the Bible,* ed. Robert Young (Grand Rapids, MI: William B. Eerdmans, 1976). There are, however, other words for purely naturalistic phenomena.

2. C. S. Lewis, *Mere Christianity* (New York: Macmillan, 1960), 140. *Mere Christianity* was originally published in 1943. *The Lion, the Witch and the Wardrobe* was published in 1950. This suggests that the figure of speech Lewis used in his nonfiction book stayed with him, to be developed further, with the same meaning, in his novel.

3. Notice that other war stories, especially from non-Christian societies, do not necessarily portray the battles as representing "good" versus "evil." In the greatest war story of them all, Homer's *Iliad,* there are "good guys" among both the Greeks and the Trojans, and the moral themes in the poem do not at all line up along the two sides fighting the war.

4. See Christopher Mitchell, *The Song of Songs,* Concordia Commentary (St. Louis: Concordia Publishing House, 2003), 313.

5. See his autobiography *Surprised by Joy: The Shape of My Early Life* (New York: Harcourt Brace Jovanovich, 1956), 83–100. See also *The Voyage of the Dawn Treader* (New York: Collier Books, 1970), 1–2, 69–71.

Chapter 7

1. Michael Ward, "Through the Wardrobe: A Famous Image Explored," *Seven*, 15 (1998): 55–71.
2. Michael Ward, "Escape to Wallaby Wood: Lewis's Depictions of Conversions," in *Lightbearer to the Shadowlands: The Evangelistic Vision of C. S. Lewis,* ed. Angus L. Menuge (Wheaton, IL: Crossway, 1997), 160–62.
3. Ibid., 161.
4. Ibid.
5. Ibid.

Chapter 8

1. See the Quest Ministry website, http://home.att.net/~questmin/sharing.html.
2. See the website, http://home.att.net/~questmin/seminar.html#fantasy.
3. Quoted in Hillel Italie, "Will Classic Epic Poem Catch on in U.S.?" Associated Press, *Milwaukee Journal Sentinel,* 26 February 2000, 6B.
4. Much of what follows is taken from my book, *Reading Between the Lines: A Christian Guide to Literature* (Wheaton, IL: Crossway, 1990), which discusses the issues in more detail.
5. See, e.g., Norma Fox Mazer's *When She Was Good,* about child abuse and running away; Francesca Block's *Weetcie Bat,* about homosexuality; and Brook Cole's *The Facts Speak for Themselves,* about murder and pederasty.
6. Sir Philip Sidney, "An Apology for Poetry," *Criticism: The Major Statements,* ed. Charles Kaplan (New York: St. Martin's Press, 1985), 132.
7. Ibid., 133.
8. Ibid., 115.
9. William Kirk Kilpatrick, *Psychological Seduction* (Nashville, TN: Thomas Nelson, 1983), 105–7. See also his title with Gregory Wolfe, Suzanne Wolfe, and Robert Coles, *Books That Build Character: A Guide to Teaching Your Child Moral Values through Stories* (New York: Simon & Schuster, 1994).
10. For further development of these points, see my book, *State of the Arts: From Bezalel to Mapplethorpe* (Wheaton, IL: Crossway, 1991), 145–61.
11. Werner Jaeger, *Paideia: The Ideals of Greek Culture,* trans. Gilbert Highet (New York: Oxford University Press, 1965), xxvii–xxviii.
12. J. R. R. Tolkien, "On Fairy Stories," *The Monsters and the Critics and Other Essays,* ed. Christopher Tolkien (Boston: Houghton Mifflin, 1984), 148.
13. Ibid.
14. C. S. Lewis, *Surprised by Joy: The Shape of My Early Life* (New York: Harcourt, Brace, & World, 1955), 179, 181.
15. Ibid., 69.
16. Ibid., 71.
17. G. K. Chesterton, *Orthodoxy* (London: The Bodley Head, 1908), 73.
18. Bruno Bettelheim, *The Uses of Enchantment: The Meaning and Importance of Fairy Tales* (New York: Knopf, 1976).
19. Ibid.

Chapter 9

1. Further thoughts of mine, in case you are interested, can be found in my foreword to Richard Abanes's book *Fantasy and Your Family: A Closer Look at The Lord of the Rings, Harry Potter, and Magick in the Modern World* (Camp Hill, PA: Christian Publications, 2002), ix–xii.
2. Ibid., 9–38, 81–103. See also Richard Abanes, *Harry Potter and the Bible* (Camp Hill, PA: Horizon Publishers, 2001).
3. Abanes, *Fantasy and Your Family*, 33.
4. The first definition of "witch" from *Webster's Ninth Collegiate Dictionary* (Springfield, MA: Merriam-Webster, 1983), 1354.
5. C. S. Lewis, *Surprised by Joy: The Shape of My Early Life* (New York: Harcourt Brace Jovanovich, 1956), 23.
6. Ibid., 36.
7. Ibid.
8. Ibid., 84.
9. Ibid., 87–100.
10. C. S. Lewis, *The Voyage of the Dawn Treader* (New York: Collier Books, 1970).
11. C. S. Lewis, "On Three Ways of Writing for Children," in *Of Other Worlds: Essays and Stories,* ed. Walter Hooper (New York: Harcourt Brace & World, 1966), 28.
12. Ibid., 29–30.
13. Ibid., 30.
14. C. S. Lewis, *Surprised by Joy*, 152.
15. J. R. R. Tolkien, "On Fairy Stories," in *The Monsters and the Critics and Other Essays,* ed. Christopher Tolkien (Boston: Houghton Mifflin, 1984), 148.
16. *Surprised by Joy*, pp. 180–181.

Chapter 10

1. Mark Greene, "Pullman's Purpose," *e.g. Magazine* (2001), The London Institute for Contemporary Christianity. Posted at http://www.licc.org.uk/articles/article.php/id/6.
2. Peter Hitchens, "This Is the Most Dangerous Author in Britain," *The Mail,* 27 January 2002, 63.
3. Peter Hitchens, "A Labour of Loathing," *The Spectator,* 18 January 2003.
4. Quoted in Hitchens, "The Most Dangerous Author in Britain," 63.
5. Quoted in "Philip Pullman & C. S. Lewis," *Facing the Challenge,* on the website of Focus Radio, Great Britain: http://www.focus.org.uk/lewis.htm.
6. Philip Pullman in *The Times,* January 2002, quoted in "Philip Pullman & C. S. Lewis."
7. Philip Pullman in the *Sunday Telegraph,* January 2002, quoted in "Philip Pullman & C. S. Lewis."
8. Hitchens, "Labour of Loathing."
9. http://www.hisdarkmaterials.org/article9.html.
10. Philip Pullman in the *Sunday Telegraph,* January 2002, quoted in "Philip Pullman & C. S. Lewis."
11. Quoted in Hitchens, "The Most Dangerous Author in Britain,"
12. Ibid.
13. "Philip Pullman & C. S. Lewis."

14. Philip Pullman in *The Times*, January 2002, quoted in "Philip Pullman & C. S. Lewis."
15. "Philip Pullman & C. S. Lewis."
16. "The Books and the Author" on the *Dark Materials* website: http://www.darkmaterials.net/index.php?p=contact.
17. Philip Pullman, *The Subtle Knife* (New York: Alfred A. Knopf, 2002), p. 208.
18. Ibid., p. 334.
19. Ibid., p. 335.
20. Philip Pullman, *The Amber Spyglass* (New York: Alfred A. Knopf, 2000), p. 441.
21. Ibid., p. 518.
22. Ibid., p. 335.
23. Ibid., p. 382.
24. Lewis develops an argument for the existence of God on the basis of the existence of morality in *Mere Christianity*.
25. C. S. Lewis, *The Screwtape Letters* (New York: Bantam Books, 1982), p. 19.

Chapter 11

1. See "Shelley, Dryden, and Mr. Eliot," in *Selected Literary Essays*, ed. Walter Hooper (Cambridge: Cambridge University Press, 1979). The remark about how the things they agree on—that is, their common faith—is far more important than their literary differences is in C. S. Lewis, *A Preface to Paradise Lost* (New York: Oxford University Press, 1961), 9.
2. See A. D. Nuttal, *The Alternative Trinity: Gnostic Heresy in Marlowe, Milton, and Blake* (New York: Oxford University Press, 1998).
3. From Blake's "The Marriage of Heaven and Hell."
4. See my article "Know Nothings" and the works and authors it references in *World Magazine*, 3 July 2004.
5. C. S. Lewis, *Preface to Paradise Lost*, 76–77.
6. John Milton, *Paradise Lost*, Book I, line 263.
7. Ibid., Book III, line 380.
8. C. S. Lewis, *Preface to Paradise Lost*, 100. And yet, as Walter Hooper points out, for all the difficulty Lewis notes in creating a good character who is more interesting than the villain, Aslan "is a million times more interesting than any of his equally convincing bad characters." [Walter Hooper, "Narnia: The Author, the Critics, and the Tale," in *The Longing for a Form: Essays on the Fiction of C. S. Lewis*, ed. Peter J. Schakel (Kent, OH: Kent State University Press, 1977), 106.]
9. C. S. Lewis, *Preface to Paradise Lost*, 101.
10. Ibid., 102.
11. Ibid., 134.
12. Ibid., 133.
13. Ibid., 130.
14. Ibid., p. 99.
15. Ibid., p. 102.
16. Greene.
17. Ibid., p. 335.
18. M. Stanton Evans, *The Theme Is Freedom: Religion, Politics, and the American Tradition* (Washington, DC: Regnery, 1996).
19. *Paradise Lost*, Book II, lines 910–919.

Chapter 12

1. C. S. Lewis, "Fern-Seed and Elephants," in *Christian Reflections*, ed. Walter Hooper (London: HarperCollins, 1981), 194.
2. For a full account of this worldview, see my book *Postmodern Times: A Christian Guide to Contemporary Thought and Culture* (Wheaton, IL: Crossway, 1994).
3. See, for example, Graham Johnston, *Preaching to a Postmodern World: A Guide to Reaching 21st Century Listeners* (Grand Rapids, MI: Baker, 2001).
4. Northrop Frye, *The Great Code: The Bible and Literature* (New York: Harvest Books, 2002).

BIBLIOGRAPHY

Abanes, Richard. *Fantasy and Your Family: A Closer Look at The Lord of the Rings, Harry Potter, and Magick in the Modern World*. Camp Hill, PA: Christian Publications, 2002.

——. *Harry Potter and the Bible*. Camp Hill, PA: Horizon Publishers, 2001.

Bettelheim, Bruno. *The Uses of Enchantment: The Meaning and Importance of Fairy Tales*. New York: Knopf, 1976.

Blake, William. "The Marriage of Heaven and Hell." In *The Norton Anthology of English Literature*. Vol. 2. Ed. M. H. Abrams, et al. 4th ed. New York: W. W. Norton & Co., 1979.

Carter, Margaret L. "Sub-Creation and Lewis's Theory of Literature." In *The Taste of the Pineapple: Essays on C. S. Lewis as Reader, Critic, and Imaginative Writer*. Ed. Bruce L. Edwards. Bowling Green, OH: Bowling Green State University Popular Press, 1988.

Chesterton, G. K. *Orthodoxy*. London: The Bodley Head, 1908.

Ditchfield, Christin. *A Family Guide to Narnia: Biblical Truths in C. S. Lewis's The Chronicles of Narnia*. Wheaton, IL: Crossway, 2003.

Evans, M. Stanton. *The Theme Is Freedom: Religion, Politics, and the American Tradition*. Washington, DC: Regnery, 1996.

Filmer, Kath. "The Polemic Image: The Role of Metaphor and Symbol in the Fiction of C. S. Lewis." In *The Taste of the Pineapple: Essays on C. S. Lewis as Reader, Critic, and Imaginative Writer*. Ed. Bruce L. Edwards. Bowling Green, OH: Bowling Green State University Popular Press, 1988.

Frye, Northrop. *The Great Code: The Bible and Literature*. New York: Harvest Books, 2002.

Gibson, Evan K. *C. S. Lewis: Spinner of Tales: A Guide to His Fiction*. Grand Rapids, MI: William B. Eerdmans, 1980.

Glaspey, Terry W. *Not a Tame Lion: The Spiritual Legacy of C. S. Lewis*. Elkton, MD: Highland Books, 1996.

Greene, Mark. "Pullman's Purpose." *EG Magazine* (2001).

Hitchens, Peter. "A Labour of Loathing." *The Spectator*, 18 January 2003.

——. "This is the Most Dangerous Author in Britain." *The Mail*, 27 January 2002.

Hooper, Walter. "Narnia: The Author, the Critics, and the Tale." In *The Longing for a Form: Essays on the Fiction of C. S. Lewis*. Ed. Peter J. Schakel. Kent, OH: Kent State University Press, 1977.

Jaeger, Werner. *Paideia: The Ideals of Greek Culture.* Trans. Gilbert Highet. New York: Oxford University Press, 1965.

Johnston, Graham. *Preaching to a Postmodern World: A Guide to Reaching 21st Century Listeners.* Grand Rapids, MI: Baker, 2001.

Kilby, Clyde S. *The Christian World of C. S. Lewis.* Grand Rapids, MI: William B. Eerdmans, 1964.

Kilpatrick, William Kirk, Gregory Wolfe, Suzanne Wolfe, and Robert Coles. *Books That Build Character: A Guide to Teaching Your Child Moral Values through Stories.* New York: Simon & Schuster, 1994.

Kilpatrick, William Kirk. *Psychological Seduction.* Nashville, TN: Thomas Nelson, 1983.

Kleinig, John. *Leviticus.* Concordia Commentary. St. Louis: Concordia Publishing House, 2003.

Lewis, C. S. *The Allegory of Love.* London: Oxford University Press, 1938.

——————. "Christian Apologetics." In *God in the Dock: Essays on Theology and Ethics.* Ed. Walter Hooper. Grand Rapids, MI: William B. Eerdmans, 1970.

——————. *The Chronicles of Narnia: The Lion, the Witch and the Wardrobe, Prince Caspian, The Voyage of the Dawn Treader, The Silver Chair, The Horse and His Boy, The Magician's Nephew, The Last Battle.* 7 Vols. New York: Collier Books, 1970.

——————. "Fern-Seed and Elephants." In *Christian Reflections.* Ed. Walter Hooper. London: HarperCollins, 1981.

——————. "It All Began with a Picture." In *Of Other Worlds: Essays and Stories.* New York: Harcourt, Brace & World, 1966.

——————. *Letters of C. S. Lewis.* Ed. W. H. Lewis. New York: Harcourt Brace Jovanovich, 1966.

——————. *Letters to Children.* Ed. Lyle Dorsett and Marjorie Lamp Mead. New York: Macmillan, 1985.

——————. *Mere Christianity.* New York: Macmillan, 1952.

——————. *Miracles.* New York: Macmillan, 1947.

——————. "On Three Ways of Writing for Children." In *Of Other Worlds: Essays and Stories.* Ed. Walter Hooper. New York: Harcourt Brace & World, 1966.

——————. *A Preface to Paradise Lost.* New York: Oxford University Press, 1961.

——————. *The Screwtape Letters.* New York: Bantam Books, 1982.

——————. "Shelley, Dryden, and Mr. Eliot." In *Selected Literary Essays.* Ed. Walter Hooper. Cambridge: Cambridge University Press, 1979.

——————. "Sometimes Fairy Stories May Say Best What's to Be Said." In *Of Other Worlds: Essays and Stories.* New York: Harcourt, Brace & World, 1966.

——————. *Surprised by Joy: The Shape of My Early Life.* New York: Harcourt Brace Jovanovich, 1956.

——————. "What Are We to Make of Jesus Christ?" In *God in the Dock: Essays on Theology and Ethics.* Ed. Walter Hooper. Grand Rapids, MI: William B. Eerdmans, 1970.

Lindskoog, Kathryn. *The Lion of Judah in Never-Never Land: God, Man & Nature in C. S. Lewis's Narnia Tales.* Grand Rapids, MI: William B. Eerdmans, 1973.

Luther, Martin. "Against the Heavenly Prophets in the Matter of Images and Sacraments" (1535). In *Luther's Works.* Ed. Helmut T. Lehmann. Philadelphia: Muhlenberg Press, 1958.

Mitchell, Christopher. *The Song of Songs.* Concordia Commentary. St. Louis: Concordia Publishing House, 2003.

Mueller, Steven P. *Not a Tame God: Christ in the Writings of C. S. Lewis.* St. Louis: Concordia Publishing House, 2002.

Nuttal, A. D. *The Alternative Trinity: Gnostic Heresy in Marlowe, Milton, and Blake.* New York: Oxford University Press, 1998.

Pullman, Philip. *The Amber Spyglass.* New York: Alfred A. Knopf, 2000.

————. "The Dark Side of Narnia." *The Guardian,* 1998.

————. *The Golden Compass.* New York: Alfred A. Knopf, 1996.

————. *The Subtle Knife.* New York: Alfred A. Knopf, 2002.

Sayer, George. *Jack: C. S. Lewis and His Times.* San Francisco: Harper and Row, 1988.

Sayers, Dorothy L. *The Mind of the Maker.* New York: Harcourt, Brace, 1941.

Schakel, Peter J. *Reading with the Heart: The Way into Narnia.* Grand Rapids, MI: William B. Eerdmans, 1979.

Tixier, Elaine. "Imagination Baptized, or, 'Holiness' in the Chronicles of Narnia." In *The Longing for a Form.* Ed. Peter J. Schakel. Kent, OH: Kent State University Press, 1977.

Tolkien, J. R. R. "On Fairy Stories." In *The Monsters and the Critics and Other Essays.* Ed. Christopher Tolkien. Boston: Houghton Mifflin, 1984.

Veith, Gene Edward. "Good Fantasy and Bad Fantasy." *The Christian Research Journal,* Volume 23, Number 1 (2000).

————. "Know Nothings." *World Magazine,* 3 July 2004.

————. *Painters of Faith: The Spiritual Landscape in Nineteenth-Century America.* Washington, DC: Regnery, 2001.

————. *Postmodern Times: A Christian Guide to Contemporary Thought and Culture.* Wheaton, IL: Crossway, 1994.

————. *Reading Between the Lines: A Christian Guide to Literature.* Wheaton, IL: Crossway, 1990.

————. *State of the Arts: From Bezalel to Mapplethorpe.* Wheaton, IL: Crossway, 1991.

Ward, Michael. "Escape to Wallaby Wood: Lewis's Depictions of Conversions." In *Lightbearer to the Shadowlands: The Evangelistic Vision of C. S. Lewis.* Ed. Angus L. Menuge. Wheaton, IL: Crossway, 1997.

————. "Through the Wardrobe: A Famous Image Explored." *Seven,* 15 (1998).

Scripture Index

Subject Index